THE ULTIMATE GUIDE TO TRAVEL THE WORLD

How to Become Location Independent to Live and Work from Anywhere

By Norbert Figueroa

FOREWORD

Hey there!

Welcome to *The Ultimate Guide To Travel The World*—and welcome to a new world order of business and travel possibilities. By purchasing this guide, you've taken an important step toward your goal of becoming location independent.

I decided to write this guide as the source I wanted to have back when I started this personal quest of traveling long term. It is focused on the personal and financial aspect of becoming location independent, including ways in which you could translate your current lifestyle and profession to have the freedom to experience different parts of the world while still making a decent living through your online "micro-business".

You'll see here that location independence can be achieved in many ways, and any of them could work for you, but the most important thing is that you find the path that suits you best and define what location independence means to you. Don't worry, I'll guide you step by step to accomplish this.

My Journey and Location Independence

As you read through the guide, you'll learn how I achieved my own location independence. I'm an architect who hit the pause button in my career in 2011 to travel the world for what I thought would be only a year-long trip. Well, more than hitting pause, I morphed the way in which I decided to approach architecture as a profession (at least for now).

After 95 countries and over 1400 days of travel, that "year-long" trip is still going strong. Along the way, I learned how to use my passion and skills to make a living without having to depend on a "regular day job." But yes, I do work on the road, and on many occasions, I do have to work a lot. But that's part of being able to live on the road. The other part is knowing how to live on a budget, which I'll also cover here.

But, this guide doesn't just feature my story as a sample. You'll also see how other like-minded travelers managed to create a location independent lifestyle for themselves by taking advantage of today's technology and resources.

So, read on, take action, and reach that lifestyle you're dreaming of.

Cheers!

Norbert Figueroa - @globotreks

TABLE OF CONTENTS

SECTION 4: LIVING THE DREAM

SECTION 5: SETTLING BACK

• • • •

IN THEIR OWN WORDS – CASE STUDIES

You'll also meet some excellent long-term travelers and location independent entrepreneurs, and learn a bit about how and why they chose to transition to a location independent lifestyle. I'll share, in their own words, the profiles of:

YOUR FREE BONUS

As a small token of thanks for buying this book, I'd like to offer a free bonus gift exclusive to my readers. Follow the link to download a series of worksheets that will help you:

- Asses your current financial status
- Calculate a payment plan to reduce your debt
- Budget properly a trip
- Keep track of your expenses on the road

You can download the free gift here:

http://www.globotreks.com/worksheets/

INTRODUCTION

The purpose of this guide is to transform your thinking about life, work, and travel. Additionally, it will provide you with a solid foundation to build an actionable plan that will set you on the path to create your own location independent lifestyle.

Several times a week I get asked the same two questions:

"How do you pay for your trips?"

"How do you make a living without a 'real job'?"

Hopefully, I'll be able to answer both of them here by sharing step by step tips on how to get started, a number of personal stories about how I did this, as well as relevant stories from other people who have done this. But basically, the answer to both questions is tied to location independence, which gives you the ability to design a lifestyle around the concept of workplace freedom.

I'll focus on how you can be financially self-sustainable anywhere in the world by either using your passions to generate income or by translating your current location-based job to a location independent job.

TWO PASSIONS, TWO PATHS?

Travel plays a significant role in my life, and so does my architectural career. When I decided to travel long term, I knew I had to make some form of convergence to start my location independent entrepreneurial life with something I was passionate about.

There are many ways to do this, and we'll cover some of them here. Whether you want to translate your current career into something you can do on the road, start a new micro-business that doesn't require much money to setup, or simply freelance on the go; I'll show you some actionable steps to develop and properly define your location independent lifestyle based on your true passions and desires. Also, I'm dedicating a section of this guide to how to plan your time abroad, so you get the most out of every cent you earn and spend on the road.

While most portions of this guide can be applied to any trip, I believe you'll get the most out of it if you're planning on traveling long-term and making a living under your own terms.

Most people let their travel and entrepreneurial dreams slip away due to fear of the unknown, what others might think, or simply because they are comfortable enough in their "uncomfortable reality;" only to find themselves later on in life with a long list of regrets. If the current path you have in life is one that doesn't appeal to you, there's no reason you should stick to it. Now, with this whole digital globalization, it is easier than ever to create individual income streams that don't depend on a single employer.

Work no longer has to define or limit your travel experience. In fact, they can go hand in hand to allow you to reach all those dream destinations you've always had on the back of your head but think are unreachable to regular people like you and me.

Every day, regular people just like you are living out their dreams of adventure and enjoying the freedom of changing their work and personal environment on a regular basis. I'll introduce you to a few of them throughout the course of this guide and show you how they got to where they are right now. You'll meet:

- *Jody Ettenberg*, a corporate lawyer who stumbled into location independence by chance after she took her first round-the-world trip.
- *Marcello Arrambide*, who took the opportunity to fund his location independence through day trading.
- *Dave Bouskill* and *Debra Corbeil*, who left the film industry lifestyle to become huge travel blogging personalities.
- *Caz* and *Craig Makepeace*, who despite all the financial obstacles they had; they didn't put a stop to their dreams of traveling the world as a family.
- *Derek Earl Baron*, who used several offline techniques to fund a location independent lifestyle in different parts of the world before turning travel itself into a business.

Plus a few well-known personalities in the travel industry including: *Todd* and *Lauren Sullivan, Gustavo Junqueira, Jenny Leonard, Kate McCulley*, and *Matt Long*.

It doesn't matter if you're a student, professional, retiree, or family with kids; location independence is more accessible today than it has ever been.

If you know how to play your cards right, this lifestyle is yours for the taking.

A FEW DISCLAIMERS

1. You have to be committed and open to change

I'll say right from the beginning that the ideas discussed in this guide will have a better chance of working if you're open to new ideas and are willing to work hard. Also, you must take responsibility of what happens in your future, good or bad. So, from now on, you're committed to define your future in your own way.

2. You must be willing to challenge the Status Quo

Whether you're dissatisfied with it or not, to change your life you must be open to challenge the status quo to change what's around you and go above and beyond it. Don't be afraid to be different!

3. I haven't figured everything out yet (actually, I'm far from that).

I'll share several mistakes I've made along the way, as well as what I learned from them. Here I'm sharing what has been relevant for me and many other location independent entrepreneurs. But of course, beyond the scope of this guide, there's an entire universe of possibilities I'm not familiar with. But, it will simply be too overwhelming to try to grasp everything. Focus is essential for success.

I'm not an expert in any kind of business, and that has both helped me and hurt me along the way. Not knowing "all the rules" allows me to think outside the box and in many cases it plays in my favor; other times, maybe not so much.

No matter which route you choose to take after reading this guide, you will still need to do some extra research to focus properly on your preferred micro-business method and travel style.

4. The target group of readers for this guide is people interested in starting a very small, online business that creates income to allow them to travel long term or become location independent.

If you already have an advanced knowledge on entrepreneurship and have a business, maybe you won't learn much more with this guide.

Still, this guide is useful to people who are looking to "break free" from their "real jobs" without necessarily having to say goodbye to their career, or to people who are fine with their career but simply want to create additional income to travel or feel more comfortable in life.

5. Creating an online micro-business is not complex, but it does take time.

I'm not sharing here any "secret sauce" for overnight success. There is no such secret sauce! Real businesses, whether small or big, take time to build if you want to build them properly. You'll need to dedicate time to research, develop plans, build projects, create sites, and gain more knowledge that will help you develop your entrepreneurial career.

6. Location independence has its ups and downs

People think that location independence means sitting on a hammock on the beach with a laptop in hand and sipping margaritas. You might do this one day, but that's a rare thing to do. Most of the time you'll be working from your hotel room, apartment, or café; and you might spend long hours working. Having said that, depending on how responsible and organized you are, you will also have the opportunity to enjoy different locations from around the world and gather experiences only this kind of lifestyle will allow you to.

If all this resonates with you, then continue reading!

SECTION 1

CHANGING THE STATUS QUO

Whatever your dreams are, start taking them very, very seriously.
– BARBARA SHER

CHAPTER 01
CHANGE MINDSET

TRANSLATING TO THE LIFE YOU WANT

Before I ask you one important question, I want to tell you a bit about the events that led me to this moment in my life. You'll see how shifting gears and changing our mindset is so important to bring the change we want in life.

It was 2010; I was in New York, chatting with one of my best friends about my work, life, and everything in between. I mentioned to her my fear of quitting my job to travel because I felt like I had no control over the reliability of creating income streams online.

She replied to me, "you might think your stable job is reliable, but have you thought about how tomorrow your boss can call you to his office and say you're fired because of the bad economy? How reliable is that? You have absolutely no control over it, no matter how good you are. On the other hand, if you own your business, *you* are in control of what you do, which in turn could reflect on how much you earn. If you need to earn more, then it is up to you to work smarter to try to bring that extra income."

Funny enough, I had already gone through that experience. At my first job as an architect in New York City, I worked hard for months on a single project, which happened to be the biggest project in the office. This was in 2007, which was followed by the housing market crash in 2008. Since my friend (the one I mentioned above) and I were the last ones to enter the firm, we were the first ones to go out. We had no control over it. Talk about the "stability" of a stable job.

Lucky enough, I found a new job a few weeks after. I was earning less than I did before, but during hiring we discussed salary and how it would be raised after "x" amount of time working for the firm, based on yearly reviews.

Turns out that never came to be. The yearly reviews came, and I performed well in them, but the promise of a raise never materialized. The excuse... it's the bad economy.

I felt stuck there, not only economically, but also professionally, so I started to look outside the firm for other means of making it on my own. I thought of searching for other architectural jobs; I looked at working part time at another store, and I even took small design gigs on the side. Anything to make ends meet.

Those design gigs were my favorite since I was in control of what I was doing, and I was able to charge what I believed was right for my work and time. I was regaining control of my economic situation.

But something else happened that I did not intend. I've always loved to travel and every time I went out and returned from a trip, I shared with my friends my experiences, pictures, and so on. At one point, the stories became repetitive every time I met with a friend, so I thought, why not share it publicly on a blog and let my friends read it there?

I started a blog with that intention, and for months it was just that, a blog where friends could read about the things I did and some tips along the way. With time, I learned that a blog could be monetized, and that's when my sort of "entrepreneurial" light bulb turned on. What if my blog could be the extra source of income I've been looking for these past few years in my (then) current job?

That's when everything changed. My mentality focused from wanting to make it in New York, to wanting to make it on my own terms. As hard as I knew it would be to make some money out of a blog, I knew that I was the one in control. I could influence better how my life would develop, not a boss who might not even care of what I do with my life.

I became even more passionate about travel, but at the same time I didn't want to leave architecture behind. This struggle made me think and zone in on *what I wanted*.

I set my mind on making a living through my blog and architectural side gigs online and offline. I would also travel the world, visiting all the architectural marvels I studied in school and dreamed of seeing one day, in addition to other sites that don't get the same worldwide recognition.

Here's where my two passions collided and fused into one world.

That was my foundation to start my location independent lifestyle. So now I ask you:

What do YOU want?

At first glance, it might seem like a small and simple question, but as simple as it may be, it is one of the most important questions to ask yourself. And to make it an even more powerful question, you have to answer it as specific as possible.

I'm almost willing to bet that the answer you have in your mind right now is not specific enough to define what you want in your location independent future.

If you just thought "I want to be location independent to be able to travel and work from anywhere in the world," well, let me tell you that it is not focused enough. There are so many things you still need to answer there, like what will you do to be location independent? How will you accomplish it? How much money you believe is necessary to become location independent? How much you want to work vs. how much you want to travel? What projects do you want to work on? What kind of lifestyle do you want to create?

Again, don't answer these with a ballpark response; be as specific as you can.

For example, "I want to create a sustainable business designing t-shirts to be sold online, that generates $2,000 a month in profit to allow me to base myself independently in Bangkok, Mexico City, and Milan, and live and travel with a comfortable budget of $50 a day."

See, there is a lot more meat in that answer to help you understand how you will get from where you are today to that. Of course, your answer will vary according to what you want, but again, be as specific and clear as possible.

The more vague you answer this question, the harder you'll make it for yourself to achieve it.

So, why don't you give it a go...

What is your purpose?

We covered the what; now we will cover the why. Why do you want to travel? Why do you want a location independent life? What do you expect from this experience?

Just as much as you need to know the *what* behind the creation of this new phase in life, you need to understand the *why* too. Think that the *what* is the vehicle and the *why* is the fuel for that vehicle. You need a strong why, or let's call it, a strong drive and passion to fuel this quest.

This drive is essential to commit to reaching the goals you have in mind and making those dreams and plans happen. Goals give you a purpose and purpose makes the whole journey even more meaningful.

Bouncing around the world can be great, but it gets old and tiresome after a while if you're just jumping for the sake of going to a new place. "Check!!!" That's why a purpose is so important. Do you want to learn something (like Buddhism, for example)? Help people along the way? Collect or create something?

Also, if your **why** or goal is tied to a specific project, it will help condition your brain into believing you will achieve that goal. When all your energy is focused on a task, that task has a greater chance of success.

Your what and why to accomplish your dreams can be anything, and you shouldn't be afraid to express them nor fear what others might think of it. As Chris Guillebeau of *The Art of Non-Conformity* says;

> *Your dreams and big ideas belong to no one but you, and you never need to apologize for or justify them to anyone.*

In my case, I have a big goal that keeps my drive and passion on fire. I want to visit all 195 United Nations recognized countries. But it is not just checking things off a list, I want to see, experience, create memories, and learn from all those places. I want to have a better understanding of the world, its history, and architecture (even though I've noticed that the more I learn about the world, the less I comprehend it). Also, I want to see first hand a lot of world architecture that I studied (and didn't study) in school.

Purposes (yes, you can have more than one purpose) can be silly or serious. They are up to you, and there's no right or wrong here; you just have to believe that is what you really want to do.

Sometimes, even destinations have a purpose we don't intend or know of, but travel is dynamic, and sometimes things develop in ways we can't explain or comprehend. For example, during the Mongol Rally, my team and I wanted to go to the Aral Sea to see the ghost ships stranded in the middle of the desert.

Unfortunately, we didn't do our proper research on how to get there. When we were just a few miles away from the ships, the dirt road disappeared and all there was between the boats and us was a few miles of loose sand and overgrown bushes.

We gave it a shot but within a few hundred feet our cars got stuck in the sand. We knew we were not going any further, so instead we turned back and settled for a few hours in the tiny village named Zhalanash, located at the end of the road. We were carrying donated toys in our car to give to kids in Mongolia, but since we were in that village with about a dozen kids marveling at our strange cars, we decided to give them some of the toys. That was not the point of our trip to the Aral Sea, but suddenly our purpose shifted to a greater good. We unintentionally brought some happiness to the kids.

So again, what is YOUR purpose?

WHY do you want to travel and be location independent?

Would this make you happy?

Will you grow from this experience?

The greatest mistake you can make in life is to be continually fearing you will make one.
– ELBERT HUBBARD

OVERCOMING FEAR AND REDUCING REGRETS

I can tell you from firsthand experience that leaving your comfort zone to travel long term can feel scary. Creating a new lifestyle to travel will come with a basket full of fear, which is part of the reason most dreams stay just like that, dreams. It is normal to fear something new, unknown, and untested to us. You feel like there are so many things that can go wrong along the way, especially in distant countries you know nothing about. While that might be true, have you thought about all the things that can go right?

Don't fear change as it is an intrinsic part of what you want to do now (that's why you are reading this book, right?).

One thing you need to be aware is that you cannot predict the future, so you shouldn't make your decisions based on what might go right or wrong in the future. Instead, you can plan to create this lifestyle based on what you know to be true now and trust that you can figure it all out as you move along. Of course, it is not all just based on trusting, you need to work hard along the way too.

Know that when you have the courage to chase and materialize a dream, it does not mean that fear is absent; instead, it means that you are managing and controlling fear.

When you learn to manage your fear, you can use it as a drive to push yourself forward to accomplish new things. For example, I've had the small fear on the back of my head of suddenly not having any money to travel more and finding myself stranded, moneyless, in the middle of a city half way from home. Well, for me to avoid this (or at least make it less probable) I use this fear to encourage myself to work harder and diversify my income streams (which we'll talk about later).

Also, fear can make you smarter (or at least make you think of alternatives) and work harder. When you fear something, you might come up with "Plan Bs" to minimize the possibility of materializing your worst fears.

So, when it comes to becoming location independent, what fears do you have and how can you manage them?

How can you confront them and make something out of them?

How is fear affecting your planning?

Answer the questions and see how you can manage your fears to concrete actionable steps towards your goal.

———————

When fear arises, head to it. Confront it. Say thank you for showing me the way!
– YOSSI GHINSBERG

———————

THE MOST COMMON REASONS WHY PEOPLE DON'T TRAVEL

There are millions of reasons why people decide not to travel long term or become location independent. I'll show you here some of the most common reasons and how you can think outside those fears and beat them.

I HAVE NO MONEY

Don't worry, I too say it from time to time, but there's one big difference; I do my best to not let that thought stop me from traveling.

You need to stop thinking that you don't have money, instead, think how can you attract and generate more money. It's only when you accept that you need to think positive rather than negative that you'll overcome this mental obstacle. Then, there's the physical obstacle of getting the actual money, right?

I'm honest when I say to you that I don't have thousands of dollars piled in my account waiting for me to spend them on travel. Not even close. But, not having a huge amount of money is not a fear that will stop me from traveling.

I wrote a post on my blog about my fears of quitting my job and the fear of not having enough money to travel. In summary, I left New York with only $18,000 for a year of travel. I didn't feel like I had enough money to travel *and* still pay my student loans on a monthly basis.

I had a plan, though, which naturally came through my fear of failing. Of those $18,000, I set aside $5,000 for my student loans and a small backup in case of emergency. In theory, that money didn't exist. The rest, $13,000, was my day to day money for a year. This clearly wasn't enough money for me to travel to all the places I wanted to go and do all the things I wanted to do, but I adjusted myself to make it work with that amount. I did my best to travel the cheapest possible – dirt-cheap backpacking.

This trip was not something I planned overnight; I worked hard on it for over a year before I left. During that time, I worked hard in not only saving money from my regular paycheck but also creating more money through my blog and other means. I made it a goal to have some income while traveling, at least enough to travel cheaply and slowly.

I made the goal of earning $1,000 per month out of the blog by the time I left (I'll get into how to monetize a blog a few chapters ahead). That hard work paid off. At the beginning of the trip, I made around $1,000 a month. Some months more, some months less. But I was ok with whatever I brought in each month since no matter what I earned, it helped offset the withdrawals from my savings account.

So, back to you... Swallow that fear of not having money and develop a healthy mentality towards achieving your dreams and working hard on how to make them possible. Take responsibility and accept that it is up to you to make this happen. If you don't have enough money, then how can YOU fix that? Stop thinking that a raise will come out of nothing; create it!

Tap on your passions to create new streams of money. Say yes to YOUR dream and figure it out as you go along to make it work. That, my friend, is what I did and look how far I've come – despite financial obstacles, among others.

It is important for you to understand that travel is not necessarily expensive; in fact, it can cost less than living in your current city if you know how to travel on a budget. I'll go more in-depth on this in Chapter 3.

MY CAREER WILL SUFFER

A lot of people assume that just because you're following your dream of long-term travel means you're throwing away your career. This is not necessarily true if you're smart about it.

Travel is not a one-way street that leads you away from your job. In fact, travel presents you with different twists, turns, and tributaries of opportunities that might lead you to something you might be passionate to work with. Like I said before, no one can predict the future, so why would you close yourself from the possibility of seeing the world just because you fear something you can't prove? Can you prove you'll lose a professional opportunity because you set out to travel? No.

Don't get me wrong; I'm not against climbing the corporate ladder. I did it for a few years, and I know people who love this lifestyle. And that's good! But, do you love it too? If you do, then I want you to ask yourself, do you really love climbing someone else's ladder or would you prefer to build and climb your own ladder?

If you chose the latter, then hopefully this guide will help you get started with it. After all, my purpose here is to help you set up your own micro-business and online presence to shift your income to location independent sources so that you can travel while still doing what you love.

Can you create the life you really want while still including the career you're passionate about?

You definitely can. Due to our standard business mentality, we think that careers have to be dependent of one location. But guess what? Today we have enough technology to allow us to follow our career while being location independent. It does require, though, a shift in mentality and understanding how things will work under these new practices.

Can you think of ways in which you can perform your job outside the office or field? If so, how different would your job and delivery of results be? Not all jobs can be fully translated to a location independent career. Instead, they require some thinking to translate the essential tasks of the profession into tasks that can be performed online and remotely.

As an example, I started my trip with the plan of traveling up to a year and then possibly return to New York to work as an architect. I still had my mind in architecture and made sure to pursue it through my trip in one way or another. I've done small design and 3D modeling gigs on the road, as well as follow a more theoretical path when I visit architectural icons around the world, to try to understand them culturally and historically.

Thankfully things have worked out since I dedicated myself to work hard by following and combining the two passions that make me happy. And to my surprise, this experience on the road has led me to discover a new world both on a personal and professional level.

Unconsciously, I created my own business based on my passions.

Lastly, there are careers you simply cannot translate to a location independent lifestyle, like for example, being a postman. While you most probably won't be able to hop around the world performing this job in every location, you can think of what makes you passionate about this job (or any job you do). Is it the people you meet? The delivery of letters and postcards? Etc... How can you translate that "passion element" and the love you have for it into something you can do on the road? Say, for example in this case; create, design, and sell unique postcards online? Create any product related to your industry? Maybe offer a service you can provide?

Tap on the passion that makes you want to do your work every day and maybe there you'll find the answer.

Having said that, not everyone who becomes a location independent professional leaves their home base with a set professional plan or goal. Some people find their work inspiration before they leave while others leave with no set plans and find their calling along the way.

Jodi Ettenberg, of LegalNomads.com, is one of those who found their calling on the road after quitting her job as a lawyer in New

York City. As Jodi puts it:

I didn't decide to become Location Independent. I quit my job to travel for a year, starting a blog. When the blog became popular, I started to receive paid offers for freelance writing, and I figured 'hey, let's see where this goes!' Seven years later, it's still going.

While she might not be practicing law in the most common form, she has found useful her career as a lawyer since she does not need to hire a lawyer for basic things like contracts or registering trademarks. She also says that "thinking of things as a lawyer would (mitigating against potential problems) does come in handy! It also means you worry a bit too much."

Jodi is just one of thousands of people who have created or redefined their professional path on the road. Recently I read the story of Jay Meistrich and how he created a startup company while traveling to 20 countries. I recommend you search for his story online for additional encouragement and inspiration, and to put some (additional) perspective on how travel, or a location independent lifestyle, is achievable and sometimes even cheaper than you might expect. And like Jay says:

I propose that a nomadic lifestyle is a productive way to build a real company.

I agree with him, but I'll share more about this in the next two chapters.

I HAVE A FAMILY, CAN'T TRAVEL WITH KIDS

With all due respect to all the families reading this, I have to say this is a load of *caca*. Even when I don't travel with kids or as a family, I can tell you without wavering that it is possible to travel long term as a family. It might take more money, more planning, and probably more comfort on the road, but still, it is possible.

It's probable you don't know any family who has done this, so you might be skeptical of what I'm saying. Let me introduce you to a few families who have been on the road for years and are living now happier than ever:

yTravelBlog.com – Caz and Craig travel with two kids and are currently road tripping Australia on a campervan.

AlmostFearless.com – Christine Gilbert travels with her husband and two kids all around the world.

FamilyonBikes.org – The Vogel family rode their bicycles 17,285 miles from Alaska to Argentina. Even their two kids loved this incredible adventure.

RaisingMiro.com – A single mom and son chronicle their nomadic adventures as they experience global education through world travel.

In case you're wondering about the kids' education… Homeschooling.

These are just a few reasons why people say they can't travel. But remember, for every myth or reason out there to not travel, there is someone who has dispelled them.

LACK OF CONFIDENCE

While this might not be right on the top of reasons why people don't travel, this is certainly around the top reasons why people don't choose to become location independent.

Most people, including myself at one point, lack the confidence that they'll be able to make such a life-changing move in their life because they don't have the skills necessary to do it, don't have the money (addressed before), fear of being wrong, fear of failing, and so on.

About a week before I left New York, I looked around my now empty room, and I couldn't help but sit on the floor and cry. "Why did I do this?", I asked myself. I had a stable job, an apartment, I was living comfortably. So why give it all away for something I have no idea if I'm going to be able to do successfully? For a brief moment I thought I had made a mistake, but after the tears had dried, I regained my confidence (even if it was a bit shaky) and pushed forward to achieve my goal. I'm so glad that "cold-feet" moment didn't stop me.

As Jenny Leonard of NeverNorth.com says:

> *The biggest part is confidence. 13 years ago I was called crazy mad to step out and do what I did. It's very isolating to believe in something that so many people tell you is wrong. When everyone is saying something like that to you, you can't help but think, "maybe they are right." So it was a huge battle with confidence, figuring out if I was doing the right thing or not. I guess who's laughing now as I've traveled to 26 countries all over the world while my college peers back home are struggling to make ends meet.*

If you don't feel like you have the confidence to do this, why not fake it? Have you heard the saying, "fake it till you make it"? I'm not asking you to be someone you're not, but why not boost your morale and confidence by believing you are capable of doing things like this? I want to recommend you to Google search and watch the video of a TEDtalk presentation by Amy Cuddy on how your body language shapes who you are. In it you'll see how you can "fake your confidence" and how you can "fake it till you become it."

I'll close this "fear section" with a quote from Chris Guillebeau;

> *The toughest obstacles most of us have to overcome are the direct result of our own fears and insecurities.*

BUT, CAN EVERYONE TRAVEL?

Let's do a reality check here with some facts. According to BBC as of 2012, the average wage in the world is $1,480 per month.

This may sound like a lot, but the truth is that wages are unequally spread within most first-world countries. So, a "few" amount of people earn a huge chunk of that global income.

About 48% of the world's population earns less than $920 *per year*, based on WorldBank's GDP averages. It is true that it will be highly improbable for them to travel, but not impossible. That again is part of the mindset, to not think it is impossible. If you still don't believe in it, a study by Professor Abhijit Banerjee of MIT shows that people who earn an average of $1 a day (yes $1), still spend about $0.40 in other things outside of food and necessary living expenses. This is just an example of no matter how much you earn; there's always a way to spend on something else, and that something else could be travel – if that's a goal.

While I still believe that nothing is impossible, the truth is that the large majority of those people living below the global GDP average simply will never be able to travel. But, since you're reading this book, I'm quite confident that you're above the global GDP average, so why not save those "$0.40" for travel?

When I traveled to Nairobi, Kenya, I met this young man working at the guesthouse I stayed in. He was a friendly guy, so one day after his shift was over, he decided to show me around the city. At the end, we went to a bar and talked about travel. He wanted to know how I'm able to travel since he wants to do it too. But, what was even more interesting to me is that even though he is not earning a lot of money (by Western standards) he has big travel goals for himself. He wants to travel around Kenya and all the countries bordering it. He is being strict with his spending by saving everything he can from his paycheck, plus, he is doing side gigs fixing things for people – whatever it may be. What I loved about chatting with him is that he didn't think his small salary was an obstacle to travel. Sure, it will take him longer to reach the goal, but he knows he will be able to reach it one day if he's persistent with it.

So, after showing you some numbers, stats and stories; all I want you to do is to stop thinking you have no money to travel. Instead, try to understand how to travel for less money and how to create more money at the same time.

THE NEW CAREER MINDSET

An important aspect of becoming location independent is having a career on the road. No, just traveling is not a career (in general), but how can you travel while still having a career or a job you love doing? I don't mean to show you quick small paying jobs you might not necessarily like to do to travel for a longer period. Instead, what if you could translate your current professional passion into something that can be done from anywhere in the world?

But before we can get into any details of how you can do this, you need to ask yourself these questions:

Again, what do you want?

Professionally, what can you do for yourself instead of doing it for other people?

When it comes to becoming location independent, the most probable chance of succeeding in it is by becoming your own boss. And no, this doesn't mean you need to create the next big start-up company or hire employees, but it does mean that you will be working for yourself and not for others.

The second most common reason people don't travel is work commitment. That is understandable. Work gives you the money that will allow you to travel, but sometimes work does not give you the time to travel.

But, when it comes to working for others, do you ever think of anyone saying on their deathbed, "I wish I had spent more time in the office"? Said no one.

In fact, one of the top regrets of the dying, as found by palliative care worker Bronnie Ware is "I wish I lived life true to myself and not the life others expected of me." I would add to that, "I wish I had followed my dreams and traveled more." Just sayin'!

HOW TO KNOW IF YOU HAVE THE RIGHT MINDSET TO QUIT YOUR JOB TO BECOME LOCATION INDEPENDENT?

You might still have doubts and feel a bit clueless on this whole new career and life trajectory. But, maybe these six important questions will clarify your mind and help you see a more balanced picture of what you really want.

Try to answer as honest and detailed as you can. Remember, this is for you to make the right decision and know if and when it will be right to leave or make that change, so help yourself the most you can.

1. What is your true risk tolerance?

Comfort and security are two of the things we crave the most, but how willing are you to have a lower amount of comfort and security (or none of them) for an undetermined time after you quit your job, while you create a start-up, or while you travel?

How willing are you to sacrifice your "secure" paycheck for the unknown?

If you don't think you'll be able to tolerate this risk, then you probably shouldn't quit your job, or at least, you should start working on alternate modes of comfort and security way before you quit your job.

In my case, I started my blog way before quitting my job, so it gave me a moderate sense of comfort since I knew I still had the option of earning some money while on the road.

2. How much money do you need for basic expenses over the next 6-12 months?

Whether you're thinking of leaving your job or not, you should still do this to understand your spending habits.

Look at the cost of the absolute essentials you need to live for this given period.

Once you've determined your risk tolerance, you need to figure out how many months of basic expenses you need to have saved to feel confident about your decision. Naturally, these expenses will vary depending on where you live, your current costs, and your social habits.

What should be in your basic expenses calculation?

You should include the following, as applicable:

- Housing Costs/Rent
- Car Payments (if you're still keeping it after quitting)
- Utilities
- Cell Phone Bill
- Three Meals a Day
- Health Insurance
- Misc.

Also worth including, should you think it is necessary:

- Going Out Expenses
- Travel Expenses

When I was living in New York (and even today), I used Mint.com to keep track of all my spending and set my saving goals. It is free and worth trying it out. Business-wise, you can try Waveapps.com. It's free and excellent to keep your business accounting up to date.

3. What are you going to do when you quit?

It is imperative that you know what will you do after you quit. Wasn't that the reason you quit in the first place? Well, you'd be surprised how many people quit yet they don't have a clear idea of what to do next, even if they had a goal in mind.

Make sure you can jump right to the task of creating something productive for your life or new business. If it's travel what you want to do, when will you start traveling after you quit? If you want to have your own business, which goals do you want to reach and how far after you quit?

If you want to start a new business; can you start it before you quit to minimize the uncertainty of your life post-quitting your job?

Do you have any short-term goals? Can you work on them before you quit?

If you just want to change your job, can you find another one before quitting?

How will you schedule your days after you quit? At what hours will you work on your business, work out, do other projects, etc.?

4. Is your decision based on emotion or necessity?

Why do you want to leave your job?

How you answer this is important. It will show you if you're just quitting to end up in a similar job in the near future or if you're looking for true change in your life.

Is it because of your work environment? Are you progressing in your current job? Are you quitting due to unhappiness or is it more superficial?

These questions will help you separate the desires to quit based on short-term emotions versus long-term unhappiness. You might regret later if you quit because you had a rough week at work, but you might be grateful of quitting because you truly felt you had to take a different path in life. In the latter, start creating an exit strategy from now.

5. Do you have a support system?

Financial support is very important, and we covered that already, but psychological support is just as important to be successful in this new path. Surround yourself with like-minded people who support your plans and ideas. Getting their approval or simply knowing that they are happy for your courage to try something new is fuel to the heart – it will push your drive to take you farther in this new quest.

If you know people who are in the same boat, try starting a mastermind group to discuss your ups and downs and help each other with ideas. It's all about encouragement and smart planning.

If you don't have this kind of people in person, try to find them online through blogs and sites that deal with the same situations you're going through. If you're planning on traveling long term, follow and get to know people who are doing it. Ask them questions and socialize with them. Use them as your inspiration and source of knowledge.

Try to avoid spending time with nay-sayers and gatekeepers, as they will probably bring you and your plans down with their words and negativity. They probably don't understand it, so it is up to you to educate them to understand your idea better. And if it doesn't work, keep them on the sidelines for the moment.

For example, my mother thought I was crazy for quitting my job to travel. Of course, she's from a generation that didn't think of long-term travel as a lifestyle. Beyond that, she didn't understand my passion or knew that I had planned for this and that it wasn't a last minute decision. It took her time, but slowly she realized I wasn't crazy at all, and that I was working hard for it and being responsible in the way I was doing it. Eventually, she became my number one supporter!

6. Is the pain of staying worse than the pain of leaving?

I'll keep this one short and sweet. You will know it is the right time to quit when the pain that comes with the thought of staying becomes worse than the pain of leaving.

Think of these six main questions, answer them honestly. and you'll see whether quitting is the right move for you or if you should stick to your job, at least for now.

The people who get on in this world are the people who get up and look for the circumstances they want, and if they can't find them, make them.
– GEORGE BERNARD SHAW

READY TO GET STARTED? AKA, CHANGING THE STATUS QUO

We've gone through this "changing mindset" mode that is necessary for people who want to become location independent yet are not sure about it or don't believe they can achieve it. Now, changing your mindset can be useless if you don't clearly define it after the transformation.

Now I ask you. Do you feel like you're currently living the life you've always dreamed of? If your answer is yes, then close this guide now and simply email me for a refund. You don't need this guide since you're already in that "it" place in your life. But, if you answered no, then let me ask you a few more questions:

What kind of lifestyle has always appealed to you? And, why?

If you want to become location independent (whether traveling or not), what would your location independent life look like?

Think of how these answers will affect your life and the life of those who live with you (spouse, partner, and children in most cases). Should it be the case in which you have a partner that will be affected by this decision, does he/she has your same dreams and goals? Would your partner support you in this?

Ask him/her to answer the same questions you answered just now, but individually. Then, compare answers and see where you both stand. One critical thing about transitioning to a new lifestyle with a partner is that both need to be on the "same page."

Otherwise, this transition could be an uphill battle that might not have the best ending.

What is stopping you?

Ask yourself, "What is stopping me?"

List down every single reason you think is currently keeping you from getting started.

Go ahead, take your time... I'll wait here...

Done?

Ok, now let's go through the list and divide them into two important categories: Real Reasons and Perceived Reasons.

Real Reasons: These are concrete reasons that are limiting you today. For example, "I don't have enough money."

Perceived Reasons: These are reasons we think might happen and stop us from doing things. For example, "I might run out of money."

See the difference?

Now, how did your list split? Do you have more perceived reasons or actual reasons?

Let's tackle them both.

Overcoming Perceived Obstacles

Perceived obstacles are a bit more abstract to solve, since they are perceived, so they can be approached in different ways.

Work them out on your own if you're someone who already knows how to break your mental barriers and obstacles. This goes back to the "changing mindset" mode.

Work with someone to guide you through the process of breaking mental barriers. Not everyone is comfortable or believes in the power of a life coach or other personal development professional, but the trick in succeeding with them is finding the right person that has a style that suits you.

Surround yourself with people who have done or are doing what you want to achieve and break your own barriers through "osmosis." Often, when you surround yourself with like-minded people or people who have done or aspire the same things you do, you are more likely to break the tying chains and work better your problems. Social proof and community helps a lot to get inspired and driven to success.

Overcoming Actual Obstacles

Actual obstacles, while not necessarily easier to solve, they are easier to define.

You feel like you lack skills to start your own business. Why not take a course?

You feel like you don't have enough money. Why not find other ways to bring extra income? (I'll go over this later)

You don't know what to do with your current property.
Depending on your situation, would it be more beneficial to sell,
rent, or other option?

No matter what problem you have, they all, and I mean ALL,
have a way to be managed and solved.

Like Matt Long of LandLopers.com says,

> *I am not a backpacker, nor am I living off of a trust fund. I am just*
> *a normal person who has learned how to get the most out of the*
> *travel experience. I'm like many people; I have a mortgage,*
> *significant other and even three dogs, but I have also made travel*
> *my profession.*

They key is to find the best resource to manage your current
situation and to take you where you want to go both on a
professional and personal level. For example, I'm not the best
marketer or business person out there. I wanted to learn more
about managing my business, but I didn't feel like I had enough
money to pay for a course or simply have the time to allow myself
to be in one place for "X" amount of weeks to take a course. Well,
those were all excuses on my part. There is always at least one
resource. In this case, I found this website, Coursera.org, that
lists free and paid college courses from all around the world.
Courses range from digital marketing, math, music, business,
teaching, and so on. I simply took the free courses, which helped
me drastically with my management.

Again, there is a resource for everyone; it is your job to find it and
use it.

IN THEIR OWN WORDS

——— // ———

TODD & LAUREN SULLIVAN

Originally from: Australia

Website: Flightfox.com

1. What did you do before traveling (particularly to make a living) and what made you decide to become location independent?

Lauren and I had "real jobs" before becoming location independent. Lauren was a designer, then did post-grad university in international business, then spent a couple of years at a global investment fund. I was a software engineer for Defence, then did post-grad university in finance, then spent a couple of years as a private equity investor.

We enjoyed our jobs and made good money. We also planned to retire early and see the world.

Then, one day I was watching a podcast where a guy mentioned living in various cities and still working on interesting things. Instantly our entire early-retirement plan was put in question. Why work like zombies until 40 or 50 when we can just realize our dreams right now. And that was it. Over the next 6 months we left our jobs, sold everything we owned, then hit the road. I've been back to Australia for only 3 months in the last 6 years (and even then we stayed in an AirBnb).

2. How did you deal with different aspects of becoming location independent? (emotionally, socially, and financially)

We're pretty impulsive by nature, so we never did sweat that stuff. We just wanted to see the world, period. Emotionally we were liberated and excited, socially we are fairly introverted anyway, and financially we planned to launch a travel startup that we hoped would be big. We'd both left home at a young age (17), so really, this was no different. The only thing we thought about was getting everything in order to finally start our new business and hit the road for good.

3. What prompted you to choose this specific path of income and how did your previous job help you get there?

We didn't want to become location independent and start working in bars or restaurants; we still wanted to build a future and create something valuable. So our plan was to launch a travel startup. Our background in software, design and business made this the obvious choice.

That said, I was previously a backend software engineer for Defence, so that didn't translate well to building pretty websites. We paid someone else to build our first website while I spent 3-6 months getting up to speed. Also, that first website was never profitable. The blog we wrote for it was way more profitable with advertising. It took about 12 months for the blog to make enough money to finally finance our continued travel.

4. How do you evaluate your current situation (financially and emotionally) compared to your "past life"?

Emotionally, we no longer have dreams, we just have plans. In our "past life", we had dreams about things we'd do "one day" after we retired. Now, it feels like we can do anything we want. Of course we'd love to achieve certain things that seem out of reach, but we can try to achieve those things right now rather than wait. It's a strange (and liberating) feeling to have the freedom to do anything. Sometimes it's actually difficult to decide (yep, poor us, too much freedom).

Financially, there are two sides to the equation, inflows and outflows. We would have made much more money in our "past lives", but we were living in a very expensive city with a different mentally. One of the best parts about location independence is limiting your "things" to a carry-on bag. It completely changes your mentality too. You no longer want a Porsche or a new TV or anything that doesn't fit in your bag. So, in absolute terms we're worse off, but in real terms, we're much better off.

5. If you had to do it all over again, what would you change?

The only things we'd change would be business related. We'd still have left at that same time, visited the same places, met the same people, tried the same foods, etc. In a business sense, we'd have been more honest with ourselves about what people are willing to pay for. It's easy to get caught up in travel and thinking you could launch a business that will make lots of money. But when it comes to people reaching into their pockets, it's another story.

6. Is there anything else you'd like to add based on your experience?

Most of all, there's nothing to be worried about in attempting to go location independent. As long as you reserve enough money to fly home, there's always a backup plan. The risk is that you may not enjoy travel (this hits everyone at some point) or you can't earn enough money. But it's worth taking those minor risks for the endless opportunities.

CHAPTER 2

STRUCTURING LOCATION INDEPENDENCE

DEFINING YOUR LOCATION INDEPENDENCE

Before moving forward, I want to go back to the broad definition of location independence.

It is the ability to design a lifestyle around the concept of workplace freedom.

But, what kind of location independent entrepreneur you want to be? Yes, I'll be calling you an entrepreneur since I believe you're in the process of becoming one. That is if you're not one already and are simply looking to transform your business into a location independent business.

It is not enough to simply declare you want to be location independent; you need to define *exactly* what being location independent means to *you* and how you want to experience it. Once you define that, you'll be able to define further what you can do for a living, or in other words, how to structure your business. Or who knows, it could also work the other way, in which the business you create dictates your location independence. But the purpose here is to gain the greatest freedom possible.

To structure and define location independence, you need to change the work paradigm. What is a paradigm, you ask? It is the typical example of something, and in this case, it is the typical example of work that is often defined with waking up early to work in an office from 8 to 12 hours a day.

Being location independent allows you to model that paradigm and change it as necessary, so your job works for you, instead of you working for your job.

You can still wake up early and go to an office (or designated space you call an office wherever you are) and still work 8 to 12 hours a day. But you do this if you believe it is optimal and productive for you and your work. You define your working environment and vary your tasks and work hours to serve your purpose and goals, not because you have to comply with some pre-established work rules.

But, one thing must be clear; becoming your own boss requires a high degree of commitment. One of the disadvantages of being your own boss is that if you're not structured and are lazy, work never gets done since you'll always think, "Ah, I can do this later." No, you have to be as responsible, if not more responsible than when you had a boss because everything relies on you now. If you don't work, no money will come (unless you have passive streams of income).

On the other hand, you also have the power to manage your projects and decide what you need to work on to make more money in the near future. When you work for yourself, it's not about how more work is better for money, instead, how smart work is better for money.

And as you might have figured it out by now, a location independent lifestyle does require a high degree of work. As Marcello Arrambide of WanderingTrader.com puts it:

> Most people think they want this life. They think they want to have their freedom. Most people however, don't think about the work that goes into having this quality of life. It is definitely worth the risk because not everyone can live this kind of life.
> Anyone can choose to live this life and take that risk and it would be 100% worth it. Once I decided that I was going to live this new lifestyle I decided that I wouldn't give it up.

The 3 major components of a location independent lifestyle

It doesn't matter which kind of location independent lifestyle you're looking for; there are three major components that are essential to make it possible:

- **The freedom to choose where to live.** Being location independent doesn't mean you have to travel all the time or be a nomad. Sure, you can do that if you want, but location independence is achieved when you are able to choose where to live at any given point in your life without diminishing your lifestyle or needing to restart such lifestyle and income from scratch.

- **The ability to generate income through your own profitable business.** The most common approach to becoming location independent is having the power and control over your income through your own business – preferably an online based business.

- **The ability to incorporate relevant technology.** Technology has been a key factor in the recent boom of digital nomads and location independent entrepreneurs. In this globalized world, location is not so much a limiting factor, but a lack of relevant technological knowledge is.

Now we need to examine where you stand regarding these three components. This will help you define a path and prioritize and focus your efforts.

How attached are you to your current location?

As I said, being location independent doesn't necessarily mean saying goodbye to your hometown or current location. Location independence comes in different flavors, like:

- **Fully nomadic** – All the time on the road, jumping from one place to another.

- **Semi-nomadic** – You might spend all the time on the road, but you travel a lot slower and base yourself for longer periods as you go.

- **Semi-nomadic with a home-base** – You always have a home or a place to go back after your nomadic stunts.

- **Shuttling between multiple home-bases** – Your nomadic endeavors rotate between several home-bases.

No matter which style appeals you the most; you should ask yourself:

- Are you living in your current location by choice or need?
- Should you have to move out of your current location, would you still have an income or would it stop completely?

Which brings me to...

How capable are you of earning your own income (working for yourself)?

If you are still employed, how comfortable are you with someone else's decisions over your income "worthiness" and caps? And, are you really working for your dreams or someone else's?

If you already decided to take control of your income, do you know exactly how much you need to earn to live and save some money? This can vary drastically depending on the place you choose to locate yourself. Also, have you identified the means in which you'll get this new income that will eventually replace your current income?

Which also leads me to the last of the three major components...

How technologically savvy are you?

If you feel like your knowledge in technology and the web is not enough, would you like this to be the reason for you to stay put in one location? Or, would you be willing to learn more to put yourself ahead of the game. These days even YouTube can serve as a learning platform for everything, and I mean, *everything*!

On my blog I shared the story of the time I learned to drive stick shift in Morocco by just watching a Youtube video. This was *after* I rented the car and sat at a gas station completely lost not knowing what to do with it.

As I mentioned before, the key to learning is finding the right tools for you. So, do you know which are the right learning tools for you that will allow you to live location independent?

Discontent is the first necessity of progress.
– THOMAS A. EDISON

STRATEGIES TO PURSUE YOUR LOCATION INDEPENDENCE

You've decided by now that this *is* what you want to do. Well, let me congratulate you on that as that is just one of the many steps you'll take in this journey.

I'm sure you might still have a lot of questions on how to proceed. Don't worry, I will help you there, but to change the status quo you need to be sure and committed to a few things:

- You need to take full responsibility of your income and career.
- You need to be aware that in the beginning there might/will not be a guaranteed income every month.
- You need to be responsible for your own education to leverage any relevant technology that will help you be location independent and stay afloat as a business.
- You need to understand that different locations might require different approached to your work.
- And finally, you need to understand that if done properly, location should not limit your earning potential, but how smart you work will impact your earning potential.

Are we good on these terms? Good! Let's proceed by introducing you to some strategies you can use to change the status quo.

The ideas and strategies I'll discuss here are by no means new, and some of them have even been mentioned before in this guide, so you might be familiar with them already. I still recommend you to read through them because they will set the tone for subsequent sections, plus, some principle reinforcing is always good. The strategies fall into three main levels of entrepreneurship...

THREE LEVELS OF ENTREPRENEURSHIP

Now, let's start with a basic premise:

Today, it is easier to start a small online business from home that creates income without requiring a full-time job.

The fact that we have this marvelous invention called the internet, as well as a globalized economy, we can now reach a much bigger audience and serve them in way that was probably not possible just 10 years ago.

While there is a plethora of entrepreneurial ventures, these are pretty much grouped into these three categories: trading time for money, developing business systems, and creating passive income.

Each category is like a level that defines the amount of time or presence your business needs to thrive and make money. We'll start with the most basic and demanding one.

1. Trading time for money

This is the category that fits most small business owners. These can be small restaurant owners, self-employed makeup artists, freelance designers, etc.

In essence, if they are not present, no work is done or sold. Even if they have employees, the owners still have to be present to run management tasks and make sure the operation runs smoothly.

When you think of this, you're essentially trading your time for money, whether this is $10 a day or $100 an hour.

This structure is good for you if you like to be present, doing, and selling. With that in mind, however, trading time for money is often not the best way to build a *sustainable* business that will last a long time. This applies to both; location based and location independent entrepreneurs.

2. Developing business systems

This is the natural step up from trading time for money. More sustainable businesses are the ones that constantly develop systems. Now, instead of you being the one directly selling or doing, you build up a bigger business that allows for more stuff to happen without you.

These are some of the activities that represent systems development for a business:

- Writing down recurring task lists
- Focusing on any kind of business development
- Training others (employees, contractors, partners) to do specific tasks for your business
- Expansion planning
- Creating additional products
- Outsourcing

Several location independent entrepreneurs do this by hiring virtual assistants or by outsourcing tasks and projects through elance.com, fiverr.com, or other sites.

3. Creating passive income

Now, this is the apex of creating systems in your business. Passive income is the kind of income that comes in periodically no matter what you do.

But, if you have to do something for that money to come in, then it falls into one of the other two categories.

Some of the most popular examples of passive income include money from investments, rental income, and royalties, among others.

Yes, I am aware that getting these sources in the first place is not that easy, and by no mean I want to imply that it is easy to achieve passive income like this. Trust me, the last thing I want to sell here is the "piña colada dream." You know, the one where one day you're in the cubicle and the next day you're rich, sitting on the beach with a piña colada in hand. That sounds pretty, but what I want to give you are actionable steps to work smart and get closer to that "piña colada."

So, while some might earn a passive income with the sources mentioned before, truth is that most people who have a passive income to one degree or another, do it in a different way that more often than not requires a lot of work beforehand to get to where they are now.

In many cases, it can come in the form of a product. Take for example an eBook (yes, like this one you're just reading). They take a great deal of time and effort to create, but once they are done and up for sale, they can generate income for long periods of time without necessarily having to work more in order to produce more money out of it. Sure, it is not 100% passive since every now and then the author might make edits, keep an eye on performance, and other stuff; but it is a welcomed new stream of "almost passive" income nonetheless.

While passive income is the "dream" of most, you can still start and operate a business without focusing on passive income – and still succeed with it. After all, you should do what's best for your business.

But, when you think of passive income, think of it as the long-term reward that comes after serious, smart work outside your comfort zone.

———————

It is tempting to believe that the secret to happiness is less work. Here's another idea: instead of giving up on the idea of work, why not find a way to make it better?
– CHRIS GUILLEBEAU

———————

GOAL-SETTING

Setting up a micro-business doesn't require any special or technical knowledge. Most of this knowledge is either learned along the way, delegated to someone else to take care of it on behalf of you, or not necessary at all.

But, two things are extremely necessary: **hard work** and **goal setting**.

I know I already asked you to set your goals, so think of them again for a second. Would they be in line with a micro-business?

Ok, if you didn't think of your goals before, try to set them now. Don't skip this because this is for your own good. You want to start a business that creates money for you, right? Well, let's try to get this covered first.

To do that, you need some goals *of your own,* but here are a few samples.

- Earn x dollars a month with consulting
- Set up a blog to earn at least X in affiliate and advertising income
- Set up 2-3 new income sources in 1 year
- Create a small information product and generate 20 initial sales
- Diversify an online portfolio in 2 years

Well, you get the idea. Just know that the goals you set will be far more beneficial to you if they are aligned with your overall life goals. I try to stick to that, but this is not necessary for goals to be successful. In the end, it is up to you since you're the one who will be working for it.

After you create your goal list, why not refine it even more by breaking it down into measurable goals with an approximate deadline?

Common timeframes include *One-Year Goals, Five-Year Goals,* and *Lifetime Goals:*

The *One-Year Goals* are usually smaller and achievable in a matter of weeks or months. These can be revised every couple months to keep things on track.

Your *Five-Year Goals* list is for bigger things you hope to accomplish in the near future. Those goals should be revised every year or so to account for your current progress with your One-Year Goals.

Lifetime Goals are even bigger (think or really big ideas!) and could form a milestone reached through a cumulative of smaller goals. In this list, you can also add other things you want to do but don't have a specific timeline for them.

Once you have everything listed and start planning for them, you'll see how many of those goals could be achieved quicker and easier than you expected. We tend to work better when we take our ambitions seriously and focus on something that feels more tangible. We get even more encouraged to reach further when we achieve certain goals in our life.

Remember, the pathway to a location independent lifestyle begins with clearly understanding what you want to get out of life.

————————

For all of the most important things, the timing always sucks. Waiting for a good time to quit your job? The stars will never align and the traffic lights of life will never all be green at the same time. The universe doesn't conspire against you, but it doesn't go out of its way to line up the pins either. Conditions are never perfect. "Someday" is a disease that will take your dreams to the grave with you. If it's important to you and you want to do it "eventually," just do it and correct course along the way.
– TIM FERRISS

————————

IN THEIR OWN WORDS

———————//———————

MATT LONG

Originally from: United States

Website: LandLopers.com

1. What did you do before traveling (particularly to make a living) and what made you decide to become location independent?

I was a DC lobbyist for 12 years before leaving my job. I have a MA in International Relations and always meant to include travel and foreign cultures into my professional life, but my first job was in domestic politics and instead of leaving it I just stayed. I grew bored though and the occasional vacation wasn't doing enough to feed my wanderlust. So about five years ago I decided to start my site as a creative outlet. From the beginning I sort of hoped that I would be able to make it my career, but it took me a while to figure out how. I finally made the leap two and a half years ago when my previous employer and I decided to part ways.

2. How did you deal with different aspects of becoming location independent? (emotionally, socially, and financially)

Well, first I think that being location independent doesn't mean you're traveling all the time. While I could work from anywhere in the world, I do have a home; a house, partner, dogs and so on. Emotionally and socially it can be isolating, which is why I think the successful person will be a strong self-motivator. No one is around to tell you what to do, so you just have to do it. Financially we all have different paths; no two people in this career make money in the same exact way. I do a lot of different things and at the end of the day I'm essentially a freelance digital media expert.

3. What prompted you to choose this specific path of income and how did your previous job help you get there?

It chose me really. I began to realize that the skill sets I had developed as a successful blogger were valuable and rare. So I began to market them. My old 9-5 job helped me in that I also worked from home and had to really be my own boss. What helped the most though was learning how to sell and always engage with new people.

4. How do you evaluate your current situation (financially and emotionally) compared to your "past life"?

Well, emotionally I've never been better. It's scary to think how unhappy I was before and how that impacted all facets of my life. One's job is important and it's vital that we all pursue things that interest us. I've never been happier, although I've never worked harder. Financially, I actually make more now than I did as a lobbyist. I'm a firm believer that if you're happy and are doing something you enjoy (and work hard!) then the money will follow.

5. If you had to do it all over again, what would you change?

There are always things we wish we had done better, but the truth is that we learn more from mistakes than we do successes. I wouldn't change anything because I wouldn't be the person I am today. Especially in a job field that didn't exist until a few years ago, getting out there, taking chances and sometimes failing is vitally important.

6. Is there anything else you'd like to add based on your experience?

Being location independent sounds like the dream job, and it is great but it is also a job. There are no free rides in life and in order to get by everyone has to be willing to work hard. This is especially true for entrepreneurs. We have to make our own way and it's not easy, but for those of us who love it there is nothing better in the world.

SECTION 2

FINANCING LOCATION INDEPENDENCE

Twenty years from now you will be more disappointed by the things that you didn't do than by the ones you did do. So throw off the bowlines. Sail away from the safe harbor. Catch the trade winds in your sails. Explore. Dream. Discover.
— MARK TWAIN

CHAPTER 3

FINANCING LOCATION INDEPENDENCE

THE FINANCIAL IMPLICATIONS OF BECOMING LOCATION INDEPENDENT

Before I dig into the ways in which you can create money as a location independent entrepreneur, I need to tell you first the financial implications of this lifestyle. Once you have a good overview of this, you might be able to make an informed decision on which path to pursue when it comes to creating money.

As I mentioned at the beginning of this guide, one of the questions I get asked the most is, "how do you pay for your long-term trip?"

I'll rephrase that question to fit a more general audience: **How do you finance your location independent lifestyle?**

There are many ways in which you could finance it, and we'll go over them in the next section of this guide. But, they all come down to one fact: You have to take control of your finances by creating your own business or finding your way to generate an income online.

Don't get scared with the word business. In fact, let's keep calling it a micro-business since it is something you will start on your own, based on what you do already or a passion that you have.

The truth is that when you start your micro-business or any venture in which you can generate money, chances are that in the first few months (or years in some cases), you might not see any profit. That's why I recommend starting your passion business before quitting your current job. That way, you can develop something on the side while still having a secure paycheck.

Depending on what you end up building, it is possible you won't know how much money you'll bring in month to month. This side of the entrepreneurial life can be stressful since you can have months in which you make a lot of money but other months in which you barely got enough to live, or less. I had this experience when I was still living and working in NYC. I had the security of my day job's paycheck, but I could see how the income from my blog could go as high as $1,000+ a month, or as low as $200.

With experience, I got to learn more about the seasonal changes and how they affect my business (which, in this case, is my blog). For some reason, I noticed that February, August, and December tended to be slow months, but May, January, and October tended to be quite good.

It is essential to keep track of your finances and your sources of income to know how they fluctuate according to the time of the year. A pretty obvious example would be someone selling costumes online. Sales will skyrocket during September and October (Halloween), but then the rest of the year they will flat-line with a few small holiday exceptions where there might be some sales.

After you understand how your finances work, you can make informed assumptions about how could the next month(s) look and how should your life as a location independent person be.

Balancing your lifestyle with your work

I'll start with a tip I learned the hard way during my trip. If you want to operate as a real location independent business, your next moves as a nomad should be highly influenced by how your business is performing.

What do I mean? During my first and second year of travel, all I wanted was to travel, travel, travel, and see everything. Understandable, we all want to see the world. What I wasn't doing properly back then was that I didn't keep proper track of my business finances. I had some money saved, so I knew I could continue traveling for at least a year. But what I wasn't paying attention to was that I was not a sustainable traveler. It didn't matter how cheap and how affordable my trips were, I was not bringing enough money to keep up with my travel pace and the business expenses at the same time. Slowly, I spent a great part of my savings.

The third year I put a stop to that and became more conscious about my finances and work. As a full-time traveler, it is very hard to keep up with both work and travel. I tried to balance both for the first two years and honestly I feel like I failed. Yes, the blog continued, and yes, I made money while traveling full time; but it was not at the high potential I knew I could be doing.

For the latter part of my second year and third year, I decided to dedicate a few weeks or months to travel, and then a few weeks or months to focus on work. I would still do some work while traveling and would still do short trips while working, but one predominated over the other. This not only allowed me to enjoy more my trips but also to perform better at work when I truly dedicated my time to it. Again, it's not about hard work; it is about smart work.

Now I'm doing this interlocking schedule where I switch travel/work mentality every couple months, and it works for me.

Maybe this can work for you, or maybe not. It all depends on your style, your work focus, and what you want to do. You might prefer to spend an entire year based somewhere and then move slowly to another place. Or, you might want to be even more stable and feel the security of always coming back to a home base you can call home. They are all valid, but the important thing is that you test your working methods and see what works best for you.

Keeping on the same subject of work and travel, but jumping more into the financial aspect...

How much money do you need to have a nomadic location independent lifestyle?

The beauty of being location independent is the ability to choose to live in any country and work from there. In many cases, these countries can have a much lower cost of living than in your home country, or they could be higher; but in the end, the choice of where to go is in your hands.

When you want to budget and work out how much you need to live location independent, you need to first decide where you want to go and research the current costs of living and traveling in each destination on your list.

The internet is a great source of information, as you know, but I will caution you first before you head out to search the cost of living in Melbourne, for example. The information found on the internet can be either outdated or biased based on the living or travel standards of the person who wrote the article.

But, there's still hope on the internet! One resource I always recommend checking is BudgetYourTrip.com. This site shows the average cost for budget, mid-range, and luxury trips to pretty much all the countries in the world. Their averages are based on the crowd-sourced information of other travelers who have graciously shared their traveling costs. From my experience, I would still add 50% more of the amounts I see on the site since, in many cases, they tend to fluctuate on the lower end of the scale.

But, that's for traveling. What about basing yourself somewhere for a couple months? How can you budget that? The way you spend money when traveling is different to how you spend money when based somewhere. For starters, you don't pay as much for transportation, you don't pay for many sights, and your accommodation might be even cheaper. You can use the information found on blogs as a base. Just search for "cost of living in [city]" to find them, or even better, you can search online for forums or Facebook groups dedicated to expats in such city.

When it comes to forums and groups, what will help you the most is to ask very specific questions, so you get very specific answers.

Since at the time of writing I'm based in Chiang Mai, I'm in a Facebook group specifically for expats living in Chiang Mai. There, people ask questions about certain living costs, how to do X or Y in the city, or simply messages to get to meet people once they arrive. Groups and forums like this are extremely helpful since you get updated information that is often tailored to what you need since you are asking directly to people. And of course, meeting like-minded expats in a new city is always a plus.

———————————

The world is a book, and those who do not travel read only a page.
– SAINT AUGUSTINE

———————————

TRAVEL IS NOT (NECESSARILY) EXPENSIVE

There's something really important that you must understand; travel doesn't have to be expensive. In fact, travel can –and probably will– cost less per month than what you spend living at home (if you live in a major city in a developed country).

I want you to forget that mid-20th-century notion of travel; the one in which only rich people were able to vacation in luxurious and far off destinations. NO! Put that idea in the trash can and think of this. Every single destination can be traveled cheap or with a moderate budget. Every destination has an infrastructure that makes living there affordable to locals, and it is by using this infrastructure that you can manage to travel cheap. Now, getting to that destination can cost some money (i.e. airfares), but later in this guide we'll cover how to get to those places for much less than the usual or even for free!

I want to compare some costs to give you a few examples of how long-term travel can be cheaper than just living back home.

When I first moved to New York City, I paid $1550 per month only in rent for a regular one-bedroom apartment in Harlem. In theory, that is cheap for Manhattan. When I add my living expenses, it totaled over $2,000 per month, just to live. If I break that total monthly cost into a daily cost, it would be $66.66 per day.

Ok, New York is an expensive city, so that might not be fair. Let's compare instead my living expenses in Puerto Rico. My rent was $575 a month, and when I added all basic, necessary expenses, it came to around $1,400 per month – or $46.66 per day.

I'm currently (at the time of writing) based in Chiang Mai, Thailand, where I live with less than $500 a month. This includes everything from rent, food, transportation, and random stuff in between to have a good living, for the average daily cost of $15.40. As you can see, I'm experiencing a completely new city for a long term long term and living with basic comforts for much less than I used to spend in the US.

Sure, I'm based here only, but what about *traveling*. You know, moving from place to place visiting sights?

Let's take, for example, Japan, which is considered to be one of the most expensive countries in the world to travel. I spent about three weeks there, visiting Tokyo, Kyoto, Hiroshima, Osaka, and a few other places. Including all travel costs, I spent only an average of $62.53 per day. Remember, this is one of the most expensive countries to travel to, yet it is still cheaper than my daily expense in New York.

Still too expensive, you think? Let's compare a few other countries I traveled to in the past few years:

Average cost per day for my trip:

- $74.91 Hong Kong
- $70.61 New Zealand
- $69.44 Australia
- $61.91 Sri Lanka
- $53.15 China

- $48.75 Israel
- $41.37 Kenya
- $36.26 Laos
- $35.02 Tunisia
- $34.41 Indonesia
- $33.95 Egypt
- $33.39 Vietnam
- $23.15 Romania
- $20.46 Macedonia

You'll see that by default, some countries are quite expensive while others are very cheap. In all of them I did and saw everything I wanted (or at least most of it). While these are not all the countries I visited, if I hypothetically say all the countries listed above formed "my trip around the world," then the average cost per day of my trip would be $45.48.

If you want a real world example, the first three years of my trip cost an average of $55.44 per day! This includes all flights, all transportation, accommodation, food, travel insurance, replacing my iPhone twice (ouch!), and even buying a used car for the Mongol Rally.

This life on the road has been cheaper than living in New York, and not so much more expensive than living in Puerto Rico.

Could I do it cheaper? Of course! I'm a budget traveler, but I splurge on adventurous experiences. I know of travelers who can do $40, $30, and even $25 a day on average for their whole trip.

UNDERSTANDING YOUR CURRENT FINANCIAL SITUATION

Before you start anything, you need to know well where you're standing financially.

If you haven't already done this, take a moment to list all your income sources and your expenses.

In your list you should include:

Income: (list the total on a monthly basis)

- Job Income
- Investment Income
- Savings Interest
- Other Income Sources

TOTAL INCOME: $

Expenses: (list the total on a monthly basis)

- Mortgage/Rent
- Groceries
- Utility Bills (gas, water, electricity)
- Car Payment
- Petrol/Gas
- Cell Phone Bill

- Internet
- Credit card and student loan bills
- Transportation
- Dining/Eating out
- Incidental and Miscellaneous purchases (coffee, snack)
- Entertainment
- Clothes
- Savings and Pension (401K or other)

TOTAL EXPENSES: $

What would be the net amount after subtracting expenses from your income? Is it enough for you to save for your micro-business or life on the road? Will you have to cut expenses to increase that amount?

The following might seem obvious, but I'll go over it anyway. If you plan on keeping the same lifestyle or similar level, then you know that your new business must cover the total expenses you have, plus more. Should you decide to cut on your costs, then you have some wiggle room in terms of how much money your business must bring for you to live (not necessarily to be profitable).

Even if you're planning on moving to a cheaper city or reduce your spending, you should still aim to match your current income with your new business since this is a financial level you're already familiar with.

A few tips and things to consider before hitting the road:

- If you plan on being nomadic, you should already factor the cost of travel into the estimated expenses your business must cover. These include, but are not limited to flights, visas, travel insurance, and more. Should your business not be able to fulfill every cost, then you must decide which expense should be reduced or eliminated.

- When calculating your income and expenses, it is advisable for you to underestimate your income and overestimate your expenses. This is beneficial for you to adjust your spending and be prepared and comfortable in case your income happens to fall at some point.

- Don't forget to include an additional 20% to 50% to your total in the expenses list for taxes, depending on your income.

- Don't forget to include your new business expenses in your calculations. These can include business taxes and operational costs like hosting, monthly subscriptions for tools and software, payroll, and more.

- Before leaving, you should have at least six months worth of your current expenses saved in your account, in addition to at least $5,000 for any emergency or contingency (like an emergency flight, paying an apartment deposit, an unexpected hospital visit).

- You should have a guaranteed, or well estimated, income for at least six months based solely on your business performance, not your current job.

- You should understand from top to bottom how your business' finances work and how much it costs you to run it on a monthly basis.

SAMPLE COSTS OF LIVING LOCATION INDEPENDENT AND TRAVELING THE WORLD

The following samples are taken directly from my expense tracking and are based on some of the locations I traveled or based myself to work.

Chiang Mai, Thailand

Average Monthly Cost: $530

- Accommodation: $107
- Food: $249
- Transportation: $34
- Miscellaneous: $113

Notes: I based myself in Chiang Mai mostly to work. I didn't do any sightseeing, and I pretty much spent only the necessary to live decently.

Milan, Italy

Average Monthly Cost: $1,125

- Accommodation: $480
- Food: $351
- Transportation: $101
- Miscellaneous: $180

Notes: While Milan was a home base, I also did a bit of travel through the Lombardy region, which is also accounted in the average monthly cost.

Bucharest, Romania

Average Monthly Cost: $723

- Accommodation: $158
- Food: $314
- Transportation: $83
- Miscellaneous: $45

Notes: Bucharest is cheap to live in, but I spent less in accommodation by sharing a room.

Bali, Indonesia

Average Monthly Cost: $1,015

- Accommodation: $227
- Food: $374
- Transportation: $114
- Miscellaneous: $92

Notes: The apartment in Bali was cheap and in a good location. The total cost also includes trips to several places around the island and East Java.

Beijing, China

Average Monthly Cost: $1,488

- Accommodation: $250
- Food: $464
- Transportation: $333
- Miscellaneous: $106

Notes: China was more of a long trip instead of settling in just one place. The total also includes sightseeing, which is quite expensive in China.

You might see low numbers in some of these places, and while they were cheap, I didn't have to compromise on my comfort and lifestyle to save money.

All the costs shown above are from my experience, and they don't necessarily reflect what you will spend on your trip or foreign home base. Additionally, you should be aware that currency exchange rates change all the time, so in the future, these averages could be higher or lower.

While my numbers and the article linked above can have some correlation, how cheap or expensive a given country might be for you depends on your needs and what the country offers. In the next section, I'll explain how can you understand how much will you spend on your trip or new location. It's all about understanding the cost structure of a destination.

UNDERSTANDING THE COST OF DESTINATIONS

One of the most common reactions I got from people after I revealed on my blog that I traveled for three years with just over $60,000 was, "Wow, that's really cheap."

Throughout my years of travel I've come to learn that the cost of a destination should not simply be defined as "X country costs $X a day." Well, that "$X" number might be in the ballpark of what you might end up spending in the end, but the problem is that most people end up spending more than what they budget because they don't take their time to understand their destination and how costs are structured there.

When I did my cost breakdown in my previous post, I preferred not to give daily averages per country since many of them ranged outside of the norm from what a typical backpacker would spend. But, even when my daily average was abnormal for some countries, the "cost structure" still followed through according to how the destination prices things.

Also, along my trip I've traveled with several other people who also like to travel on budget and plan similar trips to mine, yet sometimes they do it much cheaper or much more expensive than mine. It's pretty much the same trip, but they have a different approach to how they spend their money in certain places. They either like to pamper or rough it a bit more than I do or look for alternatives that fit best what they are looking for out of the destination. Still, whether they were more expensive or cheaper than me, their spending followed the same "cost structure" as mine.

What is Cost Structure?

Ok, I'll explain what Cost Structure is (at least for me). This is a scale that marks the range of money (from cheap to expensive) a traveler is expected to spend on any destination's major tourism components, including but not limited to accommodation, sightseeing, food, transportation, and such; and how each component relates to the others cost wise. This helps you understand how to fit a destination into your budget properly by knowing exactly how your money is distributed in each place you visit. Different destinations approach all living and travel related costs in different ways, which means that each destination deserves its own careful analysis based on your style of travel and interests.

Websites like BudgetYourTrip.com, which I always recommend to see daily cost averages in any given country as a budget, mid-range, or luxury traveler; are only good enough to have a broad idea of general costs since it often falls short from the actual daily average you'll end up spending. But, I believe you can approach budgeting in a different way since only knowing a daily average doesn't mean that you know exactly how you'll be spending and distributing your money there.

How to understand the cost structure of a country?

I think it'll be best for me to explain it by showing some samples of actual countries. But before I go forward, I have to warn you that to understand the cost structure of a place, you need to do your proper research of that destination.

I approach cost structure by taking a look at the four major spending aspects of travel: *Accommodation, Food, Transportation, and Sightseeing/Entertainment.* Also, while cost structures don't dictate a specific amount, I'm using as a base an average daily spending between $50 and $60 to consider something to be cheap, moderate, or expensive. (This is a common daily average spending in most of the world for budget backpackers and mid-range travelers. My RTW average is $55 a day.)

We all know that Norway, Maldives, Australia, New Zealand, Singapore, and Japan are all expensive countries. *"Geez, you need a high budget for all of them!"* that's what most people say. But, if you approach your budgeting by considering the cost structure, you'll see that money is not spent the same way in all of them. Once you understand this, you could save money by making some smart decisions on how you should travel the country to fit into your budget.

Let's begin with Norway. Uff, one of the most expensive countries out there. How does it fare in the four categories?

NORWAY

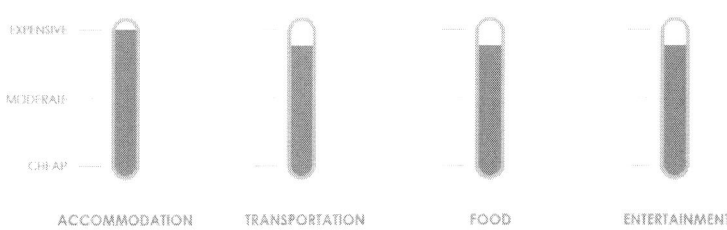

Ok, Norway is quite expensive, no doubt about that. Honestly, Norway is not a country that gives a lot of wiggle room to go cheaper unless you go very local by CouchSurfing, buying groceries, traveling slow, and focusing your sightseeing in culture (which is free in some cases). Here, quite honestly, you have to be prepared to spend a decent amount of money.

But, let's jump to the Maldives, which is as famous for its overwater bungalows as it is for its "too damn expensive" costs. Well, you might be a bit surprised by this.

MALDIVES

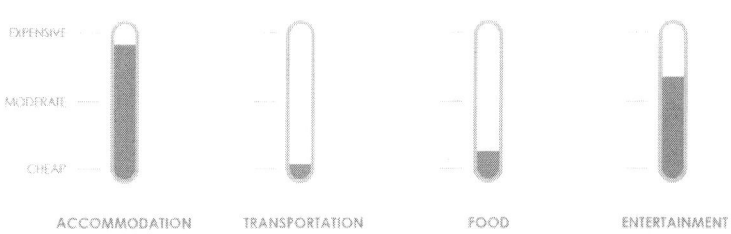

The Maldives, once reserved for luxury tourists, has now expanded extensively into the budget travel industry by offering cheap accommodation options. But beyond that, the Maldives has always offered incredibly cheap transportation and food options in its populated islands.

Let me show you a few more expensive destinations...

AUSTRALIA, NEW ZEALAND, EURO ZONE

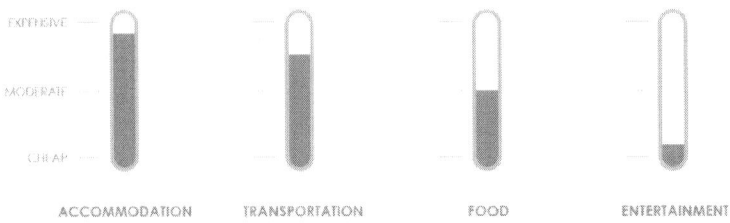

Now, how is it that Australia, New Zealand, and the Euro Zone – being expensive countries and region– can be cheap in the entertainment category? Well, you can find all sorts of prices in the entertainment category, from expensive tours to free sightseeing, but sightseeing these destinations and getting their true essence doesn't cost much since most of their sights are either free or relatively cheap.

JAPAN, HONG KONG, MACAU

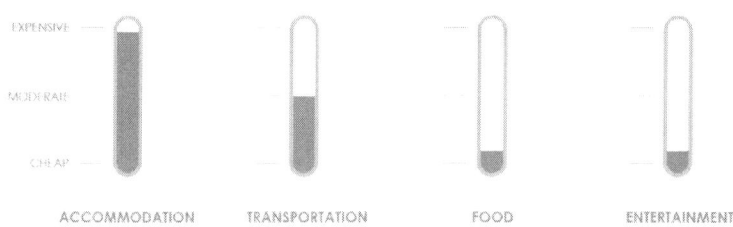

| ACCOMMODATION | TRANSPORTATION | FOOD | ENTERTAINMENT |

Just like Australia and New Zealand; Japan, Hong Kong, and Macau show their essence mostly through free or cheaply priced sights. In addition, these countries also provide you the ease of eating a good meal for a very low price, which is something Australia and New Zealand don't provide (unless you go to McDonald's and other fast-food chains). Transportation in Japan, while not the cheapest, is well organized, well connected, and moderately priced for what you get. Accommodation in these places, on the other hand, is a budget killer!

So, in most of these countries I presented above, which are considered "expensive," you could end up spending roughly the same amount of dollars per day. Should you allocate your money smartly to match your interest and how the destination structures its costs, you could make a destination much cheaper than usual.

You also have regions like Central Asia and some parts of Northern Africa and West Africa that are well known for not being necessarily cheap, but they are not budget breakers either. But, what these regions have in common is that if you plan on moving a lot, you might need to increase your budget. Places of interest in these regions are either far, remote, or don't have enough tourism to make them cheap, so there are chances you might be renting your own private transportation.

CENTRAL ASIA, WEST AFRICA

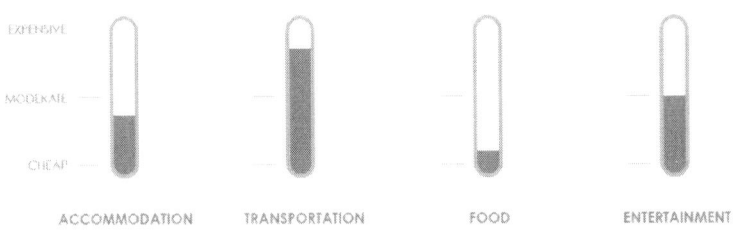

Now, let's compare other countries and regions that have a reputation of being moderately priced or cheap.

CHINA, EAST AFRICA, SRI LANKA

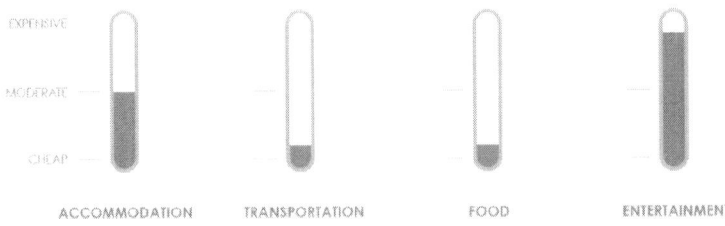

Oh, China... people say it is a cheap country, but the truth is that if you're going to sightsee a lot, prepare your budget for it. Unlike most countries, China charges you for every single site they have, and they are not cheap about it. They even charge to hike in nature... hiking!!

Regarding East Africa, the cost of food, accommodation, and transportation can be done cheaply (if you want to do it on a small budget). But just like in China, sightseeing and tours are incredibly expensive since places of interest are either remote, had to get, or there's not enough demand to offer them at lower prices.

SOUTHEAST ASIA, INDIA, EGYPT

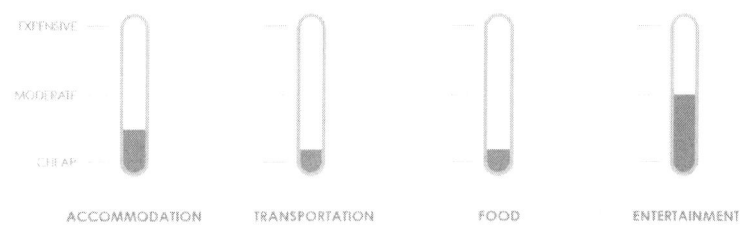

Southeast Asia still lives to its fame of being a cheap region, and so do Egypt and India. Most things can be done for cheap, but when it comes to entertainment, you might need to spend some money (not necessarily a lot) to get the most of the destination.

This list can go on and on, but I believe you get the point that destinations have a characteristic approach to pricing in each category and that once you understand their pricing, you will then know how to fit any country into your budget.

Planning a trip based on Cost Structures

Once you know where you'll go, you need to think of all or most of your actions there; like, taking the bus on a daily basis, the train from the airport, the average hostel/hotel cost under your travel style, the average meal costs, the sights you'd like to see, etc. Research them and find their costs if they are listed online so you understand how your money will be spent.

Once you do your research, you'll see several countries will have a similar cost structure. These countries can be "bundled" together to create an overall picture (or map) that will help you see how "travel" money is spent in different places around the world.

Should you be planning on doing a round the world or long-term trip, this could help you choose destinations in which you'll be comfortable with your budget. Or, discover new destinations you didn't even think you'd be able to afford, like the Maldives, for example.

If you have a budget of only $50 a day, for example, you can still travel to China, but you might need to cut on the sightseeing. Or your could go to Japan and find slower and cheaper ways to move around. Or go to Australia and focus on the free sightseeing that can be found all around the country and try to couchsurf to reduce your spending.

When people ask me how can I travel for so long and afford my trips, this is what I do. I try my best to fit the destination into my budget, and not my budget into the destination. This requires some sacrifices every now and then and missing some interesting sights, but if it is not a priority or a must, then it is not worth over spending on it.

––––––

To help you keep track of the financial aspects of planning a trip and understanding your current financial situation, I've added some bonus worksheets available to you through this link: http://www.globotreks.com/worksheets/

IN THEIR OWN WORDS

JENNY LEONARD

Originally from: United States

Website: NeverNorth.com and WhereIsJenny.com

1. What did you do before traveling (particularly to make a living) and what made you decide to become location independent?

Honestly, I never made a transition. I started out as location independent 13 years ago from day one.

I started my business straight out of college. I thought I was going to go work for an advertising agency, but when I saw how hardcore it was I opted out. (people sleeping under desks, working 80 hours a week, working your way up the ladder, etc) From there I started my own business so that I could have the freedom to pursue whatever passions I had at the time. I spent most of my childhood living in a strict house that didn't allow me to do anything that I liked doing. So the thought of working for an ad agency and not having my time to myself was like dying. I was not about to have my adulthood (where I had control of the outcome) lead me to not doing the things I wanted to do ever again.

While my passions and travel style has changed over time, my business has always been location independent.

2. How did you deal with different aspects of becoming location independent? (emotionally, socially, and financially)

The biggest part is confidence. 13 years ago I was called crazy mad to step out and do what I did. It's very isolating to believe in something that so many people tell you is wrong. When everyone is saying something like that to you, you can't help but think, "maybe they are right." So it was a huge battle with confidence, figuring out if I was doing the right thing or not. I guess who's laughing now as I've traveled to 26 countries all over the world while my college peers back home are struggling to make ends meet.

Financially it's had it's ups and downs. I've never really cared about money, more about having a good story and life experience. I've been very successful, but also had a lot of disasters happen in my life. Had I had a steady job I would shave so many absences I would likely be unemployable. Having location independence and building my own business gave me control to build what I needed and adapt it to my lifestyle and health needs. If I needed a break I could save up money and blow it all in South America (which I did. I blew 20k in 5 months traveling South America back in 2008-2009). It's just money and I can create more of it.

However, having a phat bank account is still something people look to for success. I guess adapting my measure of success. In mainstream society I'm probably seen as a failure, but for me I've had a very successful life doing things I love.

Socially, it can be isolating. People just don't get what you are doing, although these days it's more accepted.

3. What prompted you to choose this specific path of income and how did your previous job help you get there?

I didn't want to sleep under my desk and be someone's bitch. I started freelancing design because that's what I went to college for. As I ran my business I learned about what I liked, what I didn't like, what I was good at, what I sucked at and just continued to move forward and adapt my business to me. I've never had a real job so I have no previous skills to bring over. It probably would have been easier to have someone's systems to work off of in the beginning though. I had to learn everything the hard way and develop my own way of doing stuff.

4. How do you evaluate your current situation (financially and emotionally) compared to your "past life"?

I don't think I have a good comparison for this one? I've been doing it for 13 years... I've only been traveling full time for the last 4 though, but before that I would take long extended trips that were months long and the rest of the time work from a 'base'

So technically my past life was when I was a teenager living at my parents' house?

5. If you had to do it all over again, what would you change?

I would have spent time chasing the dream clients I actually wanted instead of clients who paid me. I would have spent a few months thinking and working on the strategy behind the business, what kind of clients I wanted, what my business processes and client on boarding would be and made documents and processes for it.

Then I would have done ANYTHING possible including working for free to get 3 case studies of dream clients. Then I would use those 3 case studies to sell my business and the kind of projects/work I wanted to work on.

In short, work smarter not harder.

6. Is there anything else you'd like to add based on your experience?

I think the first lab report [I wrote] on Never North might be useful for you. (You can find it at http://nevernorth.com/lab-report-april-2014/)

CHAPTER 4
CREATING MONEY ONLINE

TACTICS TO CREATE MONEY ONLINE

Getting on the path to location independence can be done in many ways, and here I'll discuss some of the most common tactics along with some stories from several people who have done it and had success with it.

While there are a lot of different tactics and ideas listed below, in general, there are two main strategies on how to work with them:

Strategy 1: Pick one thing and do it well.

This is the conventional advice; "find what works for you and stick to it. Ignore everything else."

Obviously, this is not bad advice. If that one thing you picked works for you, use it. Yet, this might not be the right approach for everyone, especially for people who are unsure about what to do or don't have the right amount of focus to do just one thing.

Strategy 2: Start doing a lot of things, and see what ends up working.

Think of this approach as juggling. At first, you might juggle your time and effort among several projects. But after a while, you will let fall the balls that are not working properly or don't suit your needs and keep juggling the ones that do work.

It's ok to let a few balls drop to the floor; it doesn't mean you failed. You're just concentrating on what matters and what works for you and your needs.

In the long-run, though, this strategy might not take you as far as the "do one thing" strategy since you might not fully focus on something to optimize it the best way possible. But on the other hand, you're putting your eggs in different baskets so you have diversity and can test what works and what not among them. Also, it's possible that this strategy could help you generate some revenue fairly quick.

Now that we've gone over the two general strategies, I want to go over the three main branches in which your business tactics can fall into.

These branches offer different approaches to working remotely or working for yourself. Each of them, though, can help you in one way or another into translating your working passion into something you can do from the road.

Remote Work/Telecommuting

If you happen to work in an industry that allows you to work from home, and more importantly a boss who understands the concept and trust you as an employee, remote work might be your easiest introduction to the location independent lifestyle.

Why is this the easiest "entry level"? You already have a job that is secure to some extent, so you don't have to look for any new leads or create something from scratch. You can simply establish the work agreement with your boss and start working either from home or other distant location.

Depending on the type of job and the agreement established, you might be asked to work during the same business hours of your workplace and maybe to check in at the office once in a while.

While this might be the easiest path to taste location independence, it is often hard to get the "blessing" from your boss to do it. Most employers shun this practice since they prefer to have direct contact with their employees and often believe working from home is not productive. But, sometimes, if you have a valid and convincing reason to do it, some employers are willing to give it a try.

When I was working in NYC, one of my coworkers had a problem with the extension of his working visa. Not wanting to lose his job, he asked my (then) boss if he could work from his home, in Greece. He was allowed to do it with the condition that his productivity would be kept at the same level and that he would work at the same work hours of the office. This meant he would work from 4 pm until 1 am to be able to communicate regularly with everyone else in the office.

Remote work is a good starting option, and many of the strategies presented in this guide will aid a remote worker to be more productive and have more time for themselves, but this should not be your primary target if you're really looking forward to a flexible location independent lifestyle.

How to approach remote working

Now, how do you approach this? First of all, you need to know the working policies of your job. Do they even accept this in the first place?

Look and ask around to see if someone else in the company is doing it or has done it in the past. How successful was their remote working? Were the employers pleased with the dynamics?

If it hasn't happened before, and you don't know your work place's policy, approach an employer (better if you already have a good relationship with them) and discuss this possibility for yourself.

But, don't ask to become a remote worker just because you want to travel. This will not look good for you. Think of any good reason you should work from home and why would you be more productive there? Usually, logistics plays a big role in this, as in the case I explained before, where the working visa became the catalyst for my coworker to ask to work remotely.

If possible, and depending on your employer's acceptance, offer them a trial period where you will work from home one or two days a week. This will allow you to prove you can do this without "detaching" completely from the workplace. If you're successful, and your employer trusts your performance, gradually increase the days in which you work from home until you reach the point in which you are a full remote worker.

Online Freelancing

A freelancer is someone with a set of skills that goes into business for themselves. They choose who they work with and what they work on, mostly on a "per project" basis.

Most freelancers' work is conducted online, which allows them to do their work from pretty much anywhere in the world, as long as there's a reliable internet connection.

The most popular careers among freelancers are:

- Graphic designers
- Web developers
- Photographers
- Writers
- Programmers
- Virtual assistants
- Translators
- Social media
- Among others...

If you think your skills can be delivered in one way or another through the internet, then you can start as a freelance worker *before* you quit your job or decide to hit the road. You need to understand the ins and outs of freelance working since they are completely different from working for a boss. You also need to understand your capabilities and see how much money you can bring with your current skills and prospective clients.

Ah, yes... you need clients!

Finding clients can be easy or hard depending on how good you are as a freelancer, how outgoing you are with your networking, how much you stand out from the crowd, and of course, how good or balanced is your pricing according to each project.

You can find prospective clients through sites like elance.com, which caters to everyone looking for freelance work, including Architects and other licensed professionals who are not often associated with the location independent lifestyle.

For graphic designers, there's also 99designs.com and designcrowd.com.

Another note on freelancing... as nice as it might sound; you have to be aware that most jobs have to be completed by a set (and probably tight) deadline. From my experience, while it is good to have that income coming in, you need to be aware that there might be moments during your trip in which you will do nothing but work. So, you might find yourself for weeks in a pretty beach bungalow but not appreciate the place.

Also, when it comes to freelancing, clients are not always stable. There might be moments in which you will have several clients and projects at the same time, and others where you could be desperately searching for clients due to lack of work. This also requires some smart money management on your part to survive any possible "dry months" where there's not enough work to pay the bills.

Another form of freelancing is consulting. This is done both online and offline, but consultants "teach" or "consult" clients with very specific needs. Depending on the type of consultation, sometimes the consultant might produce concrete work while in others the consultant only shares his informed opinion on what the client needs.

In both cases, the consultant's work has to be applied or put in practice by the client. Without the client's action, the consultant's work might just not have any effect. As opposed to typical freelance jobs in which the freelancer does deliver a final product that needs no other action from the client (say, freelance photography).

Consulting is something you should only do if you're passionate about what you're willing to consult, not simply because you want to make money out of it. Depending on how you approach it, consulting can be not that different from a regular job in which your income is based on the trade of time for money (as discussed before in Chapter 2). Still, the upside of consulting is that you can charge what you feel you are worth and what you deliver on an hourly basis (for example, $50 per hour), and scale your prices accordingly on the amount of work you have.

Should you have too many clients and can't deal with their demand, instead of downgrading your quality of work to try to deliver to all of them, you can raise or double your hourly rate to try reduce the amount of clients without losing your average income. In some cases, this tactic even helps to give yourself a raise. To see a sample story of how someone travels the world and makes a living consulting, I recommend you visit Shannon

O'Donnell's blog, ALittleAdrift.com, where she tells her story as a traveling SEO consultant.

Still, depending on your interest, there could be a better business model for you in which you could integrate your freelance and consulting skills and possibly reach even bigger masses and generate bigger results. This would be the next category...

Online Micro-Business Platform

More possibilities and options are created when you develop your online business platform. What is this, you ask?

An online business platform is a medium you choose to communicate and solve your audience's problems and fulfill their needs.

The most common approach for a business platform is a blog, but that is *not* the only online business platform out there. With today's technology, you can reach, entertain, and teach your audience through audio, video, text, social media, and more. These can be published in platforms like YouTube, Facebook, Twitter, iTunes, and WordPress, to name a few.

No matter which medium you choose to use, you still need to rely on a solid and well-designed website where your audience will not only be able to find your content, but also consume it, and reach you with ease.

For example, a very popular website I follow is the smartpassiveincome.com by Pat Flynn. Pat does two podcasts, publishes written content, and does the occasional video to complement his posts. While the podcast might be hosted on iTunes and the videos on YouTube, ultimately, his site is the place where everything is gathered together and organized cohesively to create the whole brand, communicate with his audience, and offer some products.

These days, just putting up a blog is *not* enough to guarantee some success. A blog or website might be one of the platforms to reach an audience, but you need to offer something people are willing to buy from you or deliver content that is relevant and relatable to your audience. You also need to market yourself outside your blog and niche to outreach other audiences, and with time, evolve and develop further your micro-business to adapt to the ever-changing interwebs.

I'm convinced that about half of what separates the successful entrepreneurs from the non-successful ones is pure perseverance.
– STEVE JOBS

SPECIFIC PROJECT IDEAS FOR YOUR MICRO-BUSINESS

The following are seven ideas you can explore individually or a bunch at a time (as you prefer) to start your micro-business. Each of them is presented with their pros and cons and a few quick steps to get you started:

1. CREATE AND SELL INFORMATION PRODUCTS

Information products are created to facilitate the transfer of specialized knowledge from one person to another. These can be in the form of ebooks (like this one), real books, videos, courses, podcasts, seminars, and software, to name a few.

The beauty of information products is that while they might require a great deal of work in the beginning, they can serve as a passive source of income in the long run since they can be resold again and again.

These information products, once done and on the real and/or virtual shelves, don't really need a lot of your time and input, so you can dedicate your time to creating more information products to diversify your income streams.

Of course, you need to make sure you're producing something of high quality and informative for it to be useful to the customer. Also, you need to know which would be your audience and how to market your product to them.

Here are a few good samples of this model:

- *TravelBlogSuccess.com*: Created by David Lee, it is a course that takes aspiring travel bloggers from zero to making a living out of their blog. The information might have taken a great deal of efforts to create in the beginning (and when it is updated to keep up with the industry), but in general, the money generated by new members is mostly a profit based on the original work investment.

- *UnconventionalGuides.com*: Chris Guillebeau has mastered the art of information products by creating a series of guides that can help anyone with any specific problem or need, be it becoming a freelance writer, designer, or world domination. (Yes, even world domination!)

- *MasterSketchUp.com*: Matt Donley created this site to teach people how to use SketchUp, a 3-D modeling software used in architecture and other engineering and visualization fields to represent buildings, products, or other projects. The site presents the information through e-books, videos, and regular blog posts.

As you can see, information products come in different forms and styles but I'll cover even further the three most popular forms.

eBooks: These are among the easiest to create, considering that all you need to do is create a report on Microsoft Word or other writing program, apply some design to it, and convert it into PDF.

That is the bare minimum, but you can take it a step further by designing it to look professional. If you have the skills, you can design it yourself with Photoshop or InDesign, among other software. If you know nothing about design, you can hire someone to design it for you for about $100 - $200, depending on the size of the ebook.

The upside of ebooks is that, as mentioned before, they are capable of generating a lot of money – enough money for some people to make a living exclusively out of this. But on the downside, some people don't buy ebooks since they tend not to consider self-published information worth their time and money. Also, can be a bit hard to sell if you don't have a set reputation on the topic already.

Audio & Video: These are often the next step to take if you want to offer something more than ebooks and have a product that could be slightly more interactive.

The learning curve for audio and video is higher since you need to know how to use recording software like Camtasia or similar. Camtasia, for example, allows you to either record yourself in front of the computer, record your screen (to show your step-by-step tutorial, mindmap, or PowerPoint presentation), or both at the same time.

On the upside, adding audio and video can help you raise the price of your product since the perceived value of multimedia is higher and you can potentially reach more people who could be more receptive to this learning style. On the downside, multimedia information products can take more time and work to create, and the learning curve is higher.

Why Information Products Work Well?

- **It's Not Duplicable** – Whatever you create, it is your own, and it will be unique. You can use that uniqueness to distinguish your product from anything else on the market.

- **High Margins** – In most cases, information products don't have a high production cost since the bulk of the product is information, which you already have. When it comes to pricing, you should price your product according to how valuable the information is, rather than how much it cost you to produce it.

- **It Can be Automated** – While the creation part is not automated, once the product is done, the selling part (from payment collection to product delivery) can be fully automated, so you don't have to deal with each sale. While that's fine to do, it is often recommended to keep a small degree of touch with your customers to learn about their experience with your product. You can do this by emailing them and either thanking them for the purchase or asking for some feedback.

- **Natural Expansion** – When you develop an information product that performs well, you'll get feedback from your customers, and they will let you know in subliminal ways what else they need. Naturally, you can create other products or improve current products to meet that need.

How to Decide on What to Create

You might know already what you want to create. Kudos to you! But if you don't, don't worry about it, I'll go through a few methods in which you can narrow down some ideas for your information product or other micro-business ideas.

Even if you have a clear idea of what you want to do, I still recommend going over these points to do a bit of a reality check on your idea. Who knows, you might realize it might need some tweaking to have better chances of success.

1: Follow Your Passion

Yes, first and foremost, follow your passion. As I've said countless times before, when you do something you're passionate about, you have better chances of succeeding, and you'll enjoy the process much more. It just makes sense to create a business on something you love. Success takes a lot of time and commitment, so it is better to make it easier for yourself by engaging on something you love already. Working on something you don't love pretty much defeats the purpose of working for yourself.

2: Sell What People Buy

Just because you want to create a product and have a clear idea in your mind of what it will be, doesn't mean that it will be successful. Beyond passion, successful projects thrive because you're offering something people need or want to buy. So, when thinking about a new project, forget about yourself and focus on what your potential customers want. What are their needs? Can you meet them with a product or service?

3: Ask Your Customers

This is where the first two points meet beautifully. Ask your already existing audience or reach out to potential customers through online surveys. You can create a short series of questions in which people could tell you what are their needs –

related to your business or topic. With this information, you can narrow down your "wants" (the things you have in mind to create) and their "needs" and create a product that matches on both sides.

For example, I always wanted to create a guide for round the world planning. Sure, a lot of people have done it, so why should I create another one? I tried to find a narrower focus or niche about that entire topic and for a while I struggled to find it. Then, I got recommended to check my inbox and see which where the common questions I received from readers. After some forensic analysis, I realized that the most common pain my readers had was *money*; and not just money, but how to be sustainable on the road and how to make money on the road. Their needs overlapped part of my wants, and that became this guide.

There's one important thing I have to mention about this surveying technique, though. Sometimes, people might confuse what they need with what they want, which doesn't necessarily translate the same when it comes to purchasing a product. I might want a fancy car, but I don't need a fancy car, so it doesn't matter how well that fancy car is made and marketed, chances are I'm not going to buy it.

How do you sell information products?

If you want to automate the process of receiving payments and delivering the product, you should host your information product with a seller or eCommerce platform. A seller platform is a site that once your visitor clicks the "buy now" link on your site, they will be taken there to process the payment and dispatch the product straight to the customer's email or through a download link. Sometimes the process is seamless, and the customer won't notice they left your site, in other cases not so much.

Common seller platforms in which you can host your digital information products are e-Junkie.com, 1ShoppingCart.com, and Clickbank.com.

While 1ShoppingCart might be the most professional looking of the three I mentioned, it is also the most expensive to maintain with a monthly fee that starts at $34. On the other hand, eJunkie only charges $5 a month to have your products on their eCommerce platform.

In all platforms you can price your product according to what you think is worth paying and have an affiliate program of your own, which allows you to create unique links to give to other bloggers or marketers to help sell the product for you, in exchange of a commission payment. When it comes to digital products, the recommended commission for your affiliates ranges between 30% to 50%.

Why so high? Once they are done, digital products don't require any additional production cost per sale, plus a high commission will encourage people to promote the product for you, which is a win-win situation.

———

Pros: Information products, if researched and developed properly, can bring a high-profit margin. They could become a source of semi-passive income.

Cons: They require a lot of upfront work. There's no guarantee that an information product will perform well and bring profits. They require updating now and then to keep them relevant.

―――――

TAKE ACTION:

- Decide what kind of information product you want to create
- Understand if there's a market for it
- Create the product
- Write the sales letter to be published on your blog or dedicated site for your product. This is the page potential buyers read when deciding to buy your product. You need to be convincing with this!
- Set up the order and payment logistics (I'll go over this later)
- Market the product to potential buyers through your blog, social media, and through other peers in your industry (affiliate partners).

2. BLOGGING

While a lot of people do make a decent living out of blogging, there is at least 20 times more the amount of bloggers who don't make any money blogging. So, if your main motivation behind blogging is to make money, I suggest you take alternate and easier methods. If you're in this category, feel free to skip to the next method.

Now, if you feel a passion for blogging, writing, and delivering a message; then read on. Blogging can be a very profitable platform if you're good at it, consistent, passionate, and committed to work on this in the long run. A lot of people make a living out of advertising on their blog, commissions, and sales of products, but in the great majority of cases this income came after months or even years of hard work. Usually, the initial financial payoff of a blog is from little to nothing, and even negative (since you have to pay for hosting if you're looking to become a professional blogger). This is when most people get frustrated and quit. Part of the art of blogging is patience and perseverance.

Ways to make money with a blog

Throughout the years, I've learned that there's a fine line between blogging for money and blogging for your readers. So here I'll tell you my thoughts on the various methods I know and have used, and the pros and cons about them regarding money and your audience.

AdSense

Some people might have the best intentions to have the best content for their readers, but they populate their blog with a lot of Google AdSense ads, which, in general, are not pretty and can become obtrusive to the reading experience.

I've never liked AdSense, so I don't place it on my blog. Their payouts are extremely low (unless you have an incredible amount of traffic and people click on your ads) and they are often distracting by not blending well with the site's design. Don't get me wrong. It's fine if you want to use AdSense to make a few dollars (or a couple thousands if you're lucky), but it is simply not my cup of tea.

Selling Links

This is often known as the "easy" option of making money with a blog. Basically, it is through sponsored content and links placed on your blog. A company will ask to place a link to their site on your blog, and for this, you must charge them an advertising rate. The rate depends on your niche, your traffic, your domain authority, and a few other factors; so it is hard for me to say how much you should charge. But, I'll say that for beginners, you shouldn't charge less than $100 or $150 per link per year.

Never sell permanent links! Why? Not all sites/advertisers follow Google's terms and often they do what is called Black-Hat SEO (Search Engine Optimization). These sites are often caught red-handed and penalized, and often, they trace the people who linked to them and possibly penalize them too for engaging in that practice. A term specific link reduces the possibility of getting involved in any possible "bad linking" in the long run. Plus, it is *your* site, so you have the control over it by only renting a tiny space on it for a while, not selling that space forever.

While this can be easy money, you should be careful about the amount of sponsored content you place on your blog. Once your readers start receiving too many sponsored posts or see too many paid links on your site, they will lose their trust on you and stop reading your blog. After all, you're placing stuff on your blog just for money, not because you care.

To balance this, you should only place sponsored content that you believe in, matches your niche, and that you think will serve well to your audience. Also, you should always have more content that comes from your passion than sponsored content.

How do you find advertisers?

You can approach this in two ways, proactive and reactive. When I started my blog, I didn't even bother with looking for advertisers, since that was not the focus nor the intention of my blog. After 5 or 6 months of blogging, I started receiving emails from advertisers looking to place their link on my blog. To be honest, I didn't know how to deal with them, so in my naïve blogging mind I gave some of them for free and for some of them I charged way too low. I learned the hard way, though.

If they don't come to you, you can go to them in two ways: exchange advertising contacts with other bloggers in your industry or join BlogAds or advertising/sponsorship networks in your industry to expose your blog even more. Of course, those networks will take a portion of your commission, but it's better than nothing! In the travel industry, you can find themidgame.com and bloggerbridge.com to sponsor content on your site.

A word of caution! I'm telling you this, so you don't fall for this scam like I did when I started. Companies are supposed to have a marketing budget, right? Well, they do. But many of them don't want to use it on bloggers, so they pose as other bloggers looking to exchange links, cross promote, or simply looking to do a guest post.

I have this rule of thumb now. If an advertiser emails me pretending to be a blogger, I look at their email address to see if it is commercial. If it is, that's a red flag. If it is a gmail address (or other email providers), I ask first to know which link they want to place on my blog. If it is a commercial link, it will be charged an advertising fee. If it is a real travel blog, it might be passed as a guest post. Another red flag comes when a "guest blogger" doesn't present their blog in their introduction email. A true blogger looks to expand their audience through guest blogging, so the first thing they do is present their blog to establish a relationship.

Affiliate Marketing

Affiliate Marketing is a type of performance-based marketing in which a business rewards an affiliate for each visitor or customer brought by the affiliate's marketing efforts. You have the opportunity to promote or recommend certain companies and products, and earn a commission if someone makes a purchase through your specific link.

Sounds easy? Well, it isn't. Most people don't know how to market or promote something in a way that makes their readers act upon their "promotion." Simply placing a link on your blog with no context won't make it.

From my experience, people react better when you're related to something you recommend and give an honest review about it. For example, I've reviewed a few products on my blog that I'm affiliated with. My perspective on the product, both positive and negative is what help people react and get to know more about the product or make a purchase.

My recommendation to you is to endorse specific stuff that are related to your niche and that you truly believe are useful to your readers. After all, you want to keep their trust, right?

Also, if you're already an established blogger and have a good readership, you can also contact the company of your product of interest (or its marketing company) and ask them for a discount code for your blog. Not only this is added value for your readers but it also helps establish a better image for your blog since you're creating real relationships with companies in your industry. People will see you as a big player.

How to find affiliate programs?

It is not hard to find affiliate programs you can join to earn commissions on any sold item through your unique links. The most common platforms are CJ.com (formerly known as Commission Junction), AffiliateWindow.com, Linkshare.com, AvantLink.com, ShareASale.com, and e-Junkie.com, among others. You can join them and look at the listed companies to see which ones are relevant to your niche. Remember, relevancy is key to succeeding with affiliate income. You can then apply to each company's affiliate program, and if approved, they will provide you with a unique link to place on your site so you can track all the click-throughs and sales.

For ebooks, most bloggers tend to use e-Junkie for their affiliate program. Once you join e-Junkie, you might need to ask the blogger to add you to their affiliate program if it is not displayed publicly in their directory.

In the case that you'd like to join an affiliate program with a company you don't see listed in any of the sites mentioned before, what you could do is Google search "[company name] affiliate program" and there you'll see whether they do have an affiliate program on their own or not.

A quick tip: Some people avoid clicking affiliate links and prefer to go straight to the site, thus not giving you the commission. So as a bonus to incentivize people buy through your link, what you can do is offer something of value (and unique to you) and after the reader makes the purchase, they can send you the receipt by email to receive your super awesome bonus.

A word of caution! Avoid affiliate programs that don't give a good return or give low commissions. How much you think you'll earn when all you get is a 3% of a $10 product? Not much! Amazon has a very popular affiliate program, which you can see in most blogs that recommend books or certain products. While the Amazon platform offers pretty much every product under the sun, they offer a low 4% to 7% commission. So, don't expect to make much from it, unless you have a huge audience. Still, you can join the Amazon Affiliate Program to take advantage of any book recommendation you make on your site.

I recommend looking for affiliate products that offer 20% to 50% commission, which in most cases is reserved to digital products, courses, and software.

Create Your Own Products

A product not only helps you make more money (potentially) but also adds value to your brand since you're offering something else that could help your audience.

Is it right to sell something on your blog? I don't see anything wrong with selling on your blog if you do it properly and if you believe your readers trust you. But, this is my philosophy, before selling anything; you should have already given a lot of value to your readers through free content and interaction. Not only this helps you become an authority within your niche, but it also helps people relate to you, thus making them more open to consider purchasing something from you. They already trust your free content, so for them, probably your paid content will be even better.

Lastly, I want to note that all the methods I mentioned above are not exclusive and can be combined as you wish. You can test and play with them; keep what works and ditch what doesn't.

HOW TO START A BLOG

Anyone can start a blog, and this statement comes from the guy who started a blog without even fully understanding what a blog is. I made a lot of mistakes on the way (which of course, helped me learn even more), but today I can help you fast-track the learning process so you can start your travel blog like a pro.

These tips are not only to help you create a good blog, but also to make it easier for you to rank faster in Google.

BREAKING GROUND

1. Select a specific niche

Travel is already a niche, but in today's blogging world, just blogging about travel might get you nowhere. You need to stand out, and it is easier to stand out if you write about something that you are passionate about. You have to identify yourself with something more specific, like: backpacking, luxury travel, foodie, movie locations, volunteering experiences, etc. (this applies to all niches)

A few good samples to look are:

- *AdventurousKate.com* – Kate focuses on solo female travel.
- *TheGreatAffair.com* – Candace shares stories and watercolor sketches she paints during her trips.
- *LegalNomads.com* – Jodi tells stories through food.

2. Create your blog's name and buy a proper .com domain

Believe or not, getting a good domain name is *really* important. If possible, it should be short, catchy, and memorable. You can be creative too by inventing your own terms, like for example, GloboTreks. Being creative is good, but sometimes it can make it harder for people to catch or remember the name properly.

For example, every time I meet people on the road and tell them my blog's name or URL, they all go, "globaltreks.com, got it!" Then I have to either correct them by spelling the URL or giving them a business card. I love my URL since it is my brand, so I don't mind.

How find a good domain?

I use GoDaddy.com to buy all my domain names, but any domain seller will do fine. A few recommendations:

- Don't have hyphens in the domain (i.e., site-domain.com) as it makes it harder for people to remember.

- Preferably buy a .com domain. That's what people remember, and it gives more search engine value to your site. Buy a .net if you have no choice. Forget about the rest... .org, .co, .info...

- Make sure no one else has something similar to yours.

3. Buy a hosting plan

While it doesn't matter where you buy your domain name, when it comes to hosting, a good server does have a great impact on your site's performance. Your hosting service will affect your site's speed and overall capacity, so you need to look for a reputable hosting company with a reliable service. Trust me, you don't want to have a mediocre host to save a few dollars a month. Not worth it.

In case you don't understand what hosting is, don't worry, I've got you covered. Look at it this way; hosting is like buying a parcel of land of the internet, and the domain is the address to your parcel of land where you'll build your house. The house is the blog you'll build. Trust me, it is not scary.

To start, I recommend BlueHost.com since they have great service, are extremely reliable, cheap, and most importantly, fast! I totally recommend them.

When you go to BlueHost, hit the big "Get Started Now" button. Simply enter the domain name you bought under "I have a domain name". If you don't have a domain, enter a new domain name under "new domain" to see if it is available. That new domain will be free for the first year.

Then, you will enter your personal and payment information. Followed by the selection of a hosting plan. I recommend starting with 12 months since it is not expensive, and it would give you enough time to play around and see if travel blogging is really for you.

4. Change domain nameservers if the hosting and domain are not from the same company.

This is very easy to do. Nameservers tell the domain where it will be hosted. It is like matching a home address (domain) with an empty lot (server) where you will build a house (site).

Your hosting server will have two nameservers (i.e., ns2187.bluehost.com), which you will find in your server's control panel. Copy those, and replace the ones your domain seller appointed originally. (GoDaddy in this sample)

5. Secure Your Social Media Handles

Get your unique screennames or handles on the most important social media platforms: Facebook, Twitter, Google+, Instagram, and Pinterest. Try keeping the same "handle" on all platforms for ease (except Google+ which uses your name).

Now we are ready to bring the site to life!!

SITE SET-UP!

6. Install WordPress through your host

WordPress.org is the most popular and best blogging platform to use these days. It is great with SEO (search engine optimization), so using it will help you considerably.

BlueHost has an easy "one click" WordPress install button, which you can find in the control panel.

Don't worry, it is easy. Just follow the steps.

7. Install Theme

Which theme you select will depend on how you approach your site and what will you do with it.

I've used a few free and paid themes on my site, but currently I'm using Genesis from StudioPress, with the Dynamik Website Builder child theme. I recommend this combination to anyone who wants a very flexible theme to customize their site's design to the smallest detail while still having a fast site.

Both of these are premium themes, so if you don't want to invest in them at the beginning, you can select a free theme from StudioPress.com, Woothemes.com, or even WordPress.org (which are often limited) and slowly move into a paid theme when you want to get more serious about it. But, whatever theme you choose, try choosing one that is responsive – mobile friendly.

8. Install the following plugins (they are all free)

Search for these plugins in the plugins section of the admin side of your site.

- **WordPress SEO by Yoast** – This is one of the best, if not the best, SEO plugins out there. It combines various plugins that take care of your permalinks, sitemaps, indexation, robots meta, RSS, internal links, and more. This plugin is very important since it will help structure your site in a way that makes it easy for Google to crawl and properly index your site. It also helps you create a keyword rich Home Title and Description, among other things.

- **Akismet** – This will reduce the Spam comments in your blog or niche site.

- **W3 Total Cache** – Google likes fast sites and this plugin will help you achieve that (if properly configured). I admit it is somewhat difficult to setup and it can even screw up your site if done wrong, but it's good to install it.

- **WP-DBManager** – Good to keep a backup of your site's database.

- **Conditional CAPTCHA for WordPress** – Akismet is good at fighting Spam, yet a lot of them squeeze through.

This plugin puts a CAPTCHA only to comments that look as spam, thus not bothering your real commenters. (you need Akismet for this plugin to work)

- **Easy Privacy Policy** – It is important to have a privacy policy if you want to have a "good standing" with Google. Sites without it get less love from search engines. This plugin takes care of it with just one click.

- **Contact Form 7** – Allows you to install a simple contact form so people can email you through your site.

- **Digg Digg** — Displays social media icons on a floating sidebar, making it easy for people to share your posts.

- **Zemanta** – places related posts at the bottom of the current post being read.

- **Comment Reply Notification** – Notifies commenters when they have a new reply to their comment. (It's a courtesy thing.)

- **FD Feedburner Plugin** — Manages your feed, your stream of new content.

HELP PUT YOUR SITE UNDER GOOGLE'S EYES

9. Register with Google Analytics

Setup a Google Analytics account to track your visitors, where your traffic is coming from, with which keywords, what do they see, how long they stay in your site, what do they click, and more.

A good study of your analytics will help you target your users with the correct content and will also tell you what works and what not on your site.

Once you create your site's account, you will need to place a unique code on your site to track your traffic and performance. Google will tell you where to put it. If you don't feel comfortable doing it, you can have a developer place it for you.

10. Register the site at DMOZ

Dmoz.org is the internet's largest directory system and is maintained by human editors. Being listed in Dmoz can give your site a boost to rank well in Google because Google uses Dmoz results in its directory. Submit you site just *once*, it might take months or years for them to list you (not kidding). Do it once and forget it. If they don't list you, don't worry.

11. Register the site with Google, Yahoo, and Bing Webmasters

Register your site with the three main search engines webmaster area to improve your site's visibility. It will help them recognize your site faster and will tell them to crawl it. Put each search engine code in your *WordPress SEO plugin*. These are:

- Google Webmaster Tools
- Bing Webmasters Tools (both for Bing and Yahoo!)

CONTENT CREATION AND FURTHER STEPS

12. Start an emailing list/newsletter

You might think that this is not essential, but look closely and you'll see that all professional bloggers do have a mailing list/newsletter. It helps deliver content you won't necessarily want to put on your blog but believe is valuable to your followers. It is also a way to keep in touch with them and keep them updated in a slightly more personal way. I use MailChimp.com, which is free, but they also have a paid version with more tools and options.

13. Create basic content pages

You should create a few pages that will help visitors know who you are (About page), get in touch with you (Contact page), and navigate the site (Sitemap, blog post page, and/or homepage).

When it comes to monetizing your blog and making a living with it, I *highly* recommend TravelBlogSuccess.com. Even though it is focused on travel, I think it applies to most niches. I also took this course, and even when I took it after blogging and monetizing my site for a while, I still learned a lot with the course. It goes into detail about monetization techniques and helps you understand some industry standards according to your blog's presence. Several big travel bloggers are members of its "closed" community and help each other with tips and suggestions on running a blog professionally or anything else related to it.

From here on, my recommendation is to keep a constant writing pace and to blog at least twice a week. Also, network constantly and get to know other travel bloggers in your niche and outside it through social media platforms (Facebook groups and Twitter are excellent for this).

The last thing I have to say is to have a *lot* of patience and *not* to give up. Getting traffic, spreading your name and brand, and monetizing the blog takes time and a lot of effort, but it is worth it if you work hard for it.

Get additional help!

Feel like this is too much information to absorb right now or don't fully understand something? Don't worry. There's a Travel Bloggers Facebook group I highly recommend you to join to ask fellow travel bloggers any question (search for it on Facebook as "Travel Bloggers"). People there are always willing to help, so hopefully I'll see you there too! Or, if I could help you with your question, shoot me an email at norbert@globotreks.com!

———

Pros: Blogs have the potential to be substantially monetized. They can become a form of passive income once well established.

Cons: It takes a lot of work to bring traffic to a blog. Most blogs don't generate any money due to poor performance, lack of work or focus, or people get frustrated along the way.

———

TAKE ACTION:

- Inform yourself with the in's and out's of blogging with sites like ProBlogger.net, CopyBlogger.com, and SocialMediaExaminer.com.
- Decide what kind of blog you want to create and what will

you write about.

- Follow the steps mentioned before to start a blog.
- Write a series of compelling posts before launching your blog.
- Continue writing regularly as you spread the word online (social media, directories, guest posts, etc.) and offline (family, friends, etc.) about your blog.
- Join any affiliate programs of interest and recommend any product highly related to your niche and that you believe is useful to your readers.
- After you have some traffic, play with other ways to monetize your blog.

3. BUILD AN INFORMATION PORTAL

Different from a blog, an information portal is a site that presents itself as an authority on a subject, but its content is created not only by the owner but also by readers and moderators.

Money is usually earned in the same ways as in a blog, but information portals tend to focus more on Google Adsense or third-party ad networks since they tend to generate a great amount of traffic.

If you still don't see the difference between a blog and an information portal, I'll present to you a few good samples:

- FlyerTalk.com: FlyerTalk, is probably the most popular resource for frequent flyers and expert travelers. The site presents news and also has a forum where people discuss technique or current flight deals. The reason FlyerTalk is so popular is because it focused on building its community over time by providing access to great content not often found in other places.

- *PeopleOfWalmart.com*: This one is just for laughs. People from all over the US submit pictures of embarrassing looking characters/people while shopping in Walmart. Their income comes mostly out of Adsense ads and similar kinds of ads.

- *ComoEuMeSintoQuando.tumblr.com*: This is a hilarious Tumblr in Portuguese where people submit gif (animated) images of hyperbolic representations of how they felt under certain common situations in their life. Like, "how I felt when my crush texted me back..." and you see an image of a dog running like crazy or something exaggerated.

- *BiddingforTravel.yuku.com*: This is a forum that helps Priceline.com users to place an informed bid on hotel rooms and plane tickets based on previous successful bids from other users. What Bidding forTravel.com does is remove the secrecy behind the bidding process to help you save money by bidding closer to the lowest possible price.

How To Create An Information Portal

I'll go briefly over this since the process of creating an information portal is quite similar to that of a blog. The difference is in the way you accept other people's submissions: either by contact form submissions, which you moderate before posting or through a forum where people can simply upload their content.

If you want to create a forum, you can Google "how to create a forum" to see the various options available, from self-hosted, to software, to free hosting. It all depends on what you'd want, the look, and feel.

For the general look of the portal, there are several "Adsense templates" you can use that are already optimized to place Adsense ads in key locations of the page. While they might work, you have to be aware that your portal might look exactly the same as hundreds of other portals. Under Google's eyes, this is not good since it could consider your site not to be beneficial to the readership, due to its lack of uniqueness. Google could penalize you and take away your organic traffic, which is not good. But, you can avoid this by either customizing the free template with some basic HTML and CSS (it's not that hard and if you're in this, in the long run, you should better learn the basics) or by buying a premium template that is easily customizable. Be unique!

———

Pros: Once there's a community of people coming back to the site, monetization becomes easy. Content can be easily submitted and published by your visitors.

Cons: Managing and moderating content submitted by people can be time-consuming. It takes work to keep people encouraged to keep submitting content.

———

TAKE ACTION:

- Inform yourself better on information portals and see what other sites are doing and how are they succeeding.

- Decide on which niche you want to concentrate on. You want to be specific and have a niche that is active (meaning, a lot of people talking about it).

- Create useful content that will bring people to your portal. Different from a blog, publish and promote your content as soon as it is ready.

- Continue creating content (from yourself and submitted content by visitors) and promoting the site to bring more traffic.

4. CREATIVE INCOME WITH ECOMMERCE (EBAY, AMAZON, CRAIGSLIST)

It is possible to make a living with these three platforms. In fact, so many people have adopted these sites so well in the last decade that they now make a six to eight figures income every year. Now, I'm not guaranteeing you'll get there, but if you're up for a bit of work, you could at least live out of this.

There are three basic strategies for creating an income with these sites:

Buy low and sell high

This is the easiest way to start selling on eBay, Amazon, and

Craigslist. You can still approach this in two different ways: buy high amounts from wholesalers and sell the units individually for a profit, or buy highly discounted items in store and sell them for their normal price.

A popular site for wholesale purchase of items is Alibaba.com. Once you purchase the items, you can sell them through your website or any of these three major sites. If you're interested in pursuing this path, I recommend listening to podcast #127 from smartpassiveincome.com that explains in detail how this technique works.

If the wholesale part scares you a bit, you can start by buying highly discounted items and selling them at their regular price. For example, if you go to your local department store, or an outlet, and see a pair of shoes 50% off, you can consider buying them to sell them on any of these sites (preferably Amazon or eBay).

But before buying them, you should check for how much that same pair of shoes is selling on those sites to see if you can make a profit out of your effort and risk. Yes, there's the risk you might not sell it immediately, or that you might break even or have some loss if there's no demand for the product. Also, you have to consider that these sites do take a percentage of the sale as a commission (Amazon up to 30%), so include that lost chunk of money in your initial potential profit calculation.

I also recommend listening to podcast #99 that goes in-depth on how to be profitable with this technique. In this podcast, Jessica and Cliff Larrew show how they are making over 6-figures in profit per year by buying low and selling high on Amazon.

I tried this strategy when I was getting rid of everything I owned to travel the world, and while I wasn't selling new items (nor buying them for selling), I was earning some money with things I didn't need. In some cases, the price in which I sold the items was close to store price. Cha-ching!

The good thing about this method is that you can just go to the store, buy a few items, and start your business immediately. But on the flip side, it can be a limited business since you can only buy so many items to start with, there's a lot of competition out there, and depending on the type of products you sell, you could have low margins. Also, this might not be the best business model to become location independent since you are tied to the merchandise you buy.

Become a specialized dealer

This is a natural step up for most people who start with "buy low, sell high." Here, instead of hunting for deals on various items, you focus on one specific item, or a few, and specialize in them. You can do this by establishing relationships with wholesalers or getting deals on products that sell well.

Both on Amazon and eBay you can see what other people are selling, what are they focusing on, how many have they sold, and for how much. You should poke around other sellers in your niche to understand your competition.

In most cases, bigger margins are obtained when you import products, whether buying them wholesale through Alibaba, other middlemen, or by creating direct relationships with the manufacturers (which will probably be in China). Direct relationships are not always easy to create, but you will get to know the contacts as you go deeper in the business and test what works and what not for yourself.

The good thing about this technique is the possibility of being more efficient by specializing in one type of product (or a few), and the potential for better margins. Also, if you're serious about your business, you can use private label products you can package and sell as your brand, thus giving you the opportunity to stand out even more and price "your" product differently. That first podcast I recommended talks about this. On the downside, the amount of work it requires might be quite high in the initial stages, which might not give you the opportunity to be location independent, until you figure all the processes and automate things. Also, competition can be fierce!

Create products and own your market

This would be another natural step up from the people who try the "specialized dealer" strategy. With the creation of your own product, while you will have more upfront work to design and produce it, you will also have bigger margins since you would be more in control of the production process and cost.

Again, this step comes after you feel comfortable with the eCommerce world and have some wholesaler relationships. Why? The initial process of designing your product can be costly.

You also must be sure you have direct contact with the manufacturer to make sure the quality is up to your standards, and the production cost is as low as possible.

Don't want to design something from scratch? Some wholesalers of private label right products will allow you to modify an existing product (add something you think it should have, change a detail, etc.), but you will have to pay for the molds and other production processes that might be incurred.

All this sounds heavy? No worries, there are much easier ways to create products to be sold on Amazon and eBay. You can create information products in multimedia form and offer them on a recurring basis through eBay, or simply list them on Amazon. We discussed the information product in detail before, so you should be familiar with them by now.

The good thing about this technique is that you will have little or no competition since you are offering a unique product. But on the other hand, it will require a lot more work and a possible high upfront cost (unless it is a digital information product).

————————

Pros: If you're good at finding bargains, you could earn a high profit per article. With several sites, there's no need to have direct contact with the products or sellers since they take care of the storing and delivery.

Cons: "Buy low, sell high" can be dependent on the location you are. There could be a degree of physical interaction with the products in the beginning. There's also the possibility of not selling everything for a profit.

———

TAKE ACTION:

- Look around your house for things you don't need and test the buy low, sell high strategy with them. This will help you get used to the process, which in truth, is very easy.

- Once you have some good feedback, branch out by starting the actual buy low, sell high. Go to outlet stores, yard sales, visit stored during their annual sales, and so on.

- When you're ready to step up, start looking for wholesale products you could sell.

- If you're willing to take it to the next level, start creating your own products.

5. GENERATE MONEY WITH YOUR PHOTOS

While you can freelance as a photographer, that's not what I'm about to suggest here. What I'm suggesting is selling your photos online and earn royalty from them. There's an enormous industry online of cheap, high-quality stock photos that people can buy to use commercially on their projects.

The idea is excellent, but before you start, I have to tell you that you need a proper camera (preferably a DSLR) and have some basic photography knowledge. When you submit your photos to sites like istockphoto.com, alamy.com, fotolia.com, shutterstock.com, and 123rf.com, to name a few, your photos are scrutinized and analyzed at 100% to look for any imperfection that might make them unusable to anyone. Now, this sounds scary, but it shouldn't. In reality, they are looking for imperfections (like, dust on the lens), or unintentional blur (out of focus), or other details that lower the image quality.

But, once your images are approved and online, every time they are sold you could earn from 15% to 60% of the royalties, depending on the site and your contract with them (exclusive, non-exclusive, etc.).

This might be a good option for passive income, especially if you love photography, but be aware that to make a decent income you need to upload hundreds, if not thousands, of top-quality pictures. Any picture you sell can give you anything from $0.20 to $20 or more, so this technique works better with high quantities of images, and of course, high quality photographs too.

Before starting, go to those sites I mentioned and take a look at their inventory to familiarize yourself with their style. See which images are popular and which ones sell the most. Pay attention and understand why are they popular. Could you replicate something like this?

After this, create an account and start submitting your work for approval. Once approved, your pictures will be there waiting to be sold over and over again.

A few tips that will help you:

Once you are familiar with the sites and selling platforms, look again at their most popular images. If they are popular, it means people are looking for them (they need those kinds of pictures). Try taking images with that same concept in mind to tap on what people currently need, instead of just uploading anything you have.

Also, tag and label properly all your images with specific keywords. You want your images to be properly targeted to the people who are looking for them.

Lastly, if you're photographing people, you may need to provide a model release. This could be complicated if you don't understand it, so to start, you could stick to objects, spaces, and landscapes.

———

Pros: Great potential for long-term royalties, especially if you build up a huge photo library over time.

Cons: Takes time to get started and to even see some income from it. It demands photographic skills and attention to detail.

———

TAKE ACTION:

- Go through the sites mentioned, familiarize yourself with them, and open an account in one or a few (maybe start with istockphoto.com and/or alamy.com).

- Understand what works with the most popular and best-selling photos and see how you can replicate that kind of photography with your skills.

- Continue to improve your photographic skills. I recommend

looking at the well put and easy to understand ebook, Getting Out of Auto by Bethany Salvon. Otherwise, there is a free MIT course on Photography and Photojournalism that might be a bit more complicated to understand than the ebook, but might be worth looking at. You can find it via Google.

- Upload your best photos and continue to take high-quality photos.

6. DESIGN AND CREATE TANGIBLE PRODUCTS

These are not digital information products or wholesale products like mentioned before. These tap more into the creative side and can be made on a per demand basis, just like a restaurant prepares food as it is ordered.

Years ago this business model was not feasible since the cost of small on-demand production was too high to make it worth it. But now, this type of production is more accessible. Sites like TeeSpring.com, SpreadShirt.com and CafePress.com let you create your own graphic designs to apply them on t-shirts, mugs, coasters, pillow cases, stickers, bags, and so on. What's best is that you don't need to keep an inventory of these items since orders are handled and delivered by each website. Of course, they will take a commission out of the price, but it's worth it considering all the logistical headaches you're avoiding.

There's also ImageKind.com, which specializes more on photographic and painting canvas. If you're an artist and like to paint or take great photographs, you can upload your art or photos to their site and people can create canvas and frames with your art to hang at their home or office. This is similar to the stock photo option, except that these pictures are printed, framed, and delivered physically to the customer.

You choose the final price of your prints and canvases based on a markup system. So, after production costs, you can choose to add as much profit as you think your prints are worth. Like with photo stocks, you get commissions from every single print sold.

———

Pros: It is a sweet alternative for creative people looking to design and create products without necessarily having to deal with the production logistics.

Cons: The on-demand type of production can still drive prices higher than what you would normally find in stores.

———

TAKE ACTION:

- Think of ways in which you could design something to be sold in CafePress, TeeSpring, SpreadShirt, ImageKind, or similar sites.

- Open an account on each site of interest.

- Upload your photos or graphic art and set your pricing (if allowed) to earn a decent profit.

- Promote your products through their platforms and your own platforms like blog, social media, newsletter, and so on.

7. CREATE A MEMBERSHIP SITE OR CONTINUITY PROGRAM

Many businesses are successful thanks to their continuity program or membership site. This is a way to get paid month after month by the same group of loyal customers who still want access to the service you provide.

While this might sound good, you must be aware that it is hard to get customers to sign up for a subscription program since they are often seen negatively. In order to fight this, you must do proper and detailed promotion and education through your site, social media channels, and outside your site to introduce your program to people and show them why would they benefit if they subscribe to it.

It is not recommended to have a continuity or subscription program if you don't have already a large following or some existing customers. In fact, only your most loyal customers are the ones who will probably sign up to your program, at first.

Here are a few samples of subscription-based websites:

- *ExpertFlyer.com*: This site offers advanced airline information not available through free travel websites. They're priced $5 or $10 a month depending on which plan you need.

- *BackersHub.com*: This is a successful online business that helps people who utilize the Kickstarter crowdfunding platform. It gives Kickstarted pricing on campaigns you missed out on, notifications of new campaigns, early bird rewards, and giveaways from Kickstarter Alumns.

- *TravelHacking.org*: This site offers a service to keep you up to date with the latest travel hacking offers, whether they are from credit card bonuses, cheap airfares, or other travel hacking techniques. The site has different monthly pricing depending on your needs.

Things you need to consider before setting up a subscription program:

- Why should customers sign up for this? (or better yet, why should someone pay you on a monthly basis for this?)
- What is the unique selling proposition (USP)?
- How will it improve their lives?

You should also have clear answers for the following logistical questions:

- What will you offer?
- How will it be provided to the customer?
- What should the price be?
- How can the customer sign up?
- Will you offer a trial period?
- How will the customer be billed every month?
- How can the customer cancel your service?
- How can customers refer other customers?

How can you create a subscription site/program?

There's software designed for this; including Membergate.com, aMember.com, and MemberPress.com, among many others.

These can be pricey, but they are recommended among the best options if you need a "powerful and flexible" member site. On the other hand, you can run a subscription site with just PayPal.com and/or 1ShoppingCart.com to keep on top of the monthly payments, while you handle the other technical aspects of the subscription site on your own (through your blog or another platform). It's a more manual process, but it will be much cheaper for you.

In your PayPal Business account, for example, you have the option to create a "subscription" button if you go to "Merchant Services" and hit "Create Buttons." After you specify the amount of money charged per month, and the duration of the subscription, you simply copy and paste the HTML code into your site to display the payment button.

A few extra things to consider:

- Make sure you offer a clear and easy cancelation policy to your prospective customers to let them know they can easily opt out at any time.
- Trial periods are great to lure people into trying the program to see what it is all about.
- Most people try the service, stick around for a bit, and then cancel, so try always to show your best content first to wow your customers and have them stick around longer.
- Try to automate as much as possible the content creation of the program so you can focus on other projects at the same time your program is running.

Pros: Great potential to add serious cash flow to a business that is already successful (this is not good for a business that has no customers yet). Gives your business a more professional and sustainable model that always has something new to offer.

Cons: Decent to strong resistance from customers to join since people don't like to be billed on a monthly basis. Occasional chargebacks through your merchant account when customers don't contact you to cancel.

———

TAKE ACTION:

- Think of your loyal customers and see if they would be willing to pay for a subscription service. Survey them if necessary with SurveyMonkey.com or Google Forms.
- Decide if a "member software" is what you need or if only PayPal (or similar) will be enough for you to build the site and bill customers.
- Plan and create the base content for your subscription site.
- Market your subscription site and show its benefits to your customers and readers.
- Continue creating high-quality content as needed to keep your customers returning for more.

I've gone through a series of micro-business options you can start on your own, online, with just a small investment, which in many cases can be less than $100 to start it up. Should you not feel confident or satisfied with any of the ideas discussed here, I recommend you read Chris Guillebeau's book, *The $100 Startup,* which goes more in-depth with the idea of starting your own business without requiring a high initial investment.

PUTTING IT ALL TOGETHER

Getting Paid

No matter what type of business you're looking to create, you need to think seriously about ways to get paid. There are a plethora of ways to get paid, and they all have their advantages and disadvantages according to the type of business you have or where you are (which is applicable to location independent businesses).

I'll go over the most common methods, so you familiarize yourself with them:

PayPal

These days, PayPal.com has become the king of online payments and is used by most companies. It is highly trusted and convenient for people and businesses that receive money from various international sources and in different currencies.

A few years ago, seeing that PayPal logo on a site might have put a few people away due to the lack of knowledge of this online payment service. Nowadays, just having the option to pay with PayPal is actually more convenient since: 1) PayPal already has a very strong reputation, and 2) PayPal's platform allows you to give refunds and also has a resolution center where you can dispute any transaction not done or fulfilled properly.

Still, you should be conscious of your market since PayPal while it is international, is not widely used in certain countries. In China, for example, while PayPal is available, people there prefer to use Alipay.com for their local payments and PayPal for their international ones. So, if you want to create a business focused on China, you might see that PayPal might not be your best choice of payment, or at least not the primary one.

But that's just a specific case. Most online entrepreneurs do accept PayPal and manage all of their sales and payments with this platform. Should you get into PayPal (which I recommend), it also allows you to create invoices. If you have to accept payments in person, PayPal also has a card swipe device that is attachable to a smartphone or tablet to accept payments in person. Even big companies, like airlines and retail stores, are now accepting PayPal payments on their site.

Of course, while PayPal is one of the best platforms for online payments, you must be aware that PayPal does charge a small commission, which is 2.9% (or lower) plus $0.30.

Is PayPal the only option for online payments?

NO. There is Google Wallet, and other similar sites like PayPal, but at the moment I don't recommend using them as the main platform since they don't have the same reputation or trust that PayPal has already. Many platforms have come and gone through the years, so you want to stick to something that is reliable and not risk your money.

Still, you can try them, but only as a secondary source or as a primary source if it is a specific situation, like the one mentioned before about China.

––––––––

Pros: It's easy to use, trusted, and integrated with most websites and businesses these days. It's easy to make payments by just knowing the "PayPal email address."

Cons: Might still have some trust issues with some people who are not comfortable making online payments. It might not look as professional as a Merchant Account (more on this soon). You pay a small fee to receive your payments.

––––––––

Bank Transfers and Wire Transfers

Some companies still prefer to make payments through bank transfers or wire transfers. Bank transfers (or direct deposit) are good for big payments (say, $500 or more), since you don't have to pay a fee like with PayPal. On the other hand, it might require a bit more work from the person or company paying you since they need your bank account number, routing number, and in some cases, your name (or business name), and the bank's name.

Wire transfers fall into the same category, but you should check with your bank if there are any fees for wire transfers, and how much. Certain banks might charge $25 to receive an international wire transfer. If the payment is substantial ($1000+), the fee might be worth taking. If it is a small payment, you might want to consider using Direct Deposit or PayPal, since the fee will be lower or nothing.

I once got annoyed with a company that only wanted to pay with international wire transfer. The payment was around $170, but after my bank (a Chase Bank Business Account, at that time) received the wire transfer and charged their fee, I had lost almost $35. From that moment on I made sure to check the merchant's payment methods before working with them in case I would have to add the payment fees I get from my bank to their invoice.

Another thing to note about bank transfers is that they are often not reflected in your account immediately. The balance might reflect in your account from 24 – 48 hours. So, if you're delivering a product, you might want to wait for the money to clear properly in your account first. Wire transfers often appear immediately.

———

Pros: A good way to get paid large sums to avoid high fees.

Cons: Bank transfers are not always immediate so the transaction might take more time. Not everyone is comfortable with bank transfers. The process and fees are not standards, so they may vary according to your bank and country of residence.

———

Merchant Accounts

After your business has grown, and you've dedicated to it full time, you might have the option of creating a Merchant Account. When it comes to growing businesses, a merchant account might be more convenient than PayPal or other online payment methods.

The problem with merchant accounts is that they take a lot of time and work to setup, and in some cases, a lot of money too since you might be required to put a deposit in your account (which can be up to $10,000+).

The upside of a merchant account is that you'll have more trust and authority as a seller, especially since you can accept credit cards directly. This is quite handy with customers who are not fond of PayPal.

A merchant account also allows you to customize your order form to match your site and create an order process (check out) that is more convenient for your products, which in turns helps increase conversion rates.

There are several companies that handle merchant accounts, but you can check Humboldt Merchant Services (hbms.com), BluePay.com, or SagePay.co.uk, to name a few.

———

Pros: Makes you look more professional and helps you gain trust and authority. Is completely customized. (These are big positives.)

Cons: It can be a hard and expensive process to setup, and there's more responsibility on you as a merchant to take care of payments.

Checks and Money Orders by Mail

Lastly, there are checks and money orders. This is a dying form of payment, but surprisingly, some companies still prefer to pay with checks (or at least have it as an option). There are companies that prefer to send the first payment as a check to "prove" your address and name are correct, and after that check is cashed, they send you subsequent payments through direct deposit.

Some people, though honestly I'd say is less than 1% nowadays, still like to pay with a check. So, why not have this option if you think it's worth it?

Should you need to accept checks, just provide your address directly to the merchant or customer and if you have to deliver a product, only do so after cashing the check.

If you're location independent, you can use a relative's address to receive your checks or get a P.O. Box you can check once in a while.

Pros: It's another option to get payments.

Cons: Not really that useful or convenient these days, especially if you're location independent.

———

To finalize this section, I'll say that you should start with a PayPal account and a checking account since these will be the most common methods of payment you'll have. Then, after your business has grown, and product sales become a major aspect of your income, then you should consider getting a merchant account.

———

It's not about ideas. It's about making ideas happen.
– SCOTT BELSKY

———

IN THEIR OWN WORDS

KATE MCCULLEY

Originally from: United States

Website: AdventurousKate.com

1. What did you do before traveling (particularly to make a living) and what made you decide to become location independent?

Before I left to travel, I worked in search engine marketing in Boston. I primarily worked on paid search, also known as the little ads you see on the side of Google. I worked both in-house for a travel booking site and I also worked on the agency level for a variety of clients. Basically, I'd write copy like, "Want your teeth to not fall out? Use [denture cream]!", evaluate how it performed, make a tiny tweak, evaluate it again, and continue...

Going location independent was always a dream of mine but I fell into it accidentally. I originally planned on traveling for seven months and then looking into moving abroad, maybe teaching English in Korea. When I came back from my travels, I realized that I was making almost enough money to live off my blog full-time, so I ramped up the advertising and just never went back to work!

2. How did you deal with different aspects of becoming location independent? (emotionally, socially, and financially)

Working online full-time means that I can't travel the way I used to ever again. I need to spend a few hours a day working, I need to check my email constantly, and if I meet a cool group of people on the road, I can't drop everything to travel with them for a few days. It's a bit isolating, especially when you're surrounded by backpackers who do nothing but explore and party. It's made me realize the benefits of having some kind of community wherever you go, whether it's with a travel companion or a small group of friends or an expat group somewhere.

3. What prompted you to choose this specific path of income and how did your previous job help you get there?

As soon as I discovered the concept of blogging back in 2002, I was hooked. Right away, I blogged nonstop and decided that my dream job was to get paid to blog about my life. Funny how things work out!

The reason why I've done so well for myself is because I've always been very serious about creating content that my audience will enjoy, and I've also taken blogging very seriously as a business. Blogging really plays to my personal strengths (writing, web, photography, social media, personality-based PR) and I love sharing a bit of my world with the world at large. In other words, I love it, I'm good at it, and I'm serious about it. That's why it's worked.

I've done a variety of freelance work in addition to blogging, but the lines are blurred because everything feeds into each other (I got a job writing about Asia travel because of my experience blogging about travel in Asia, etc.). One thing I've discovered over time is that as much as I love to write, I detest freelance writing. I don't like being at the mercy of an editor and most freelance travel writing gigs are about superficial, done-to-death topics like "Top 10 Sights in London" and "Things to Do in Vegas That Aren't Gambling."

I hadn't used my paid search skills in blogging until earlier this year, when I started running a PPC campaign leading to a page on my site with a high conversion rate and high affiliate commissions. That said, paid search taught me to be very ROI-oriented, which I am to this day.

4. How do you evaluate your current situation (financially and emotionally) compared to your "past life"?

I'm not going to lie -- it was rough financially for a long time. Just last year, I was down to $200 in my checking account and was owed more than $9,000 by clients who were late paying me. Anyone will tell you that making a living as a travel blogger is an extraordinarily difficult thing to do, not least because travel blogging doesn't have nearly the financial clout of fashion or food or mommy blogging. It wasn't until I was in my fourth year of blogging full-time that I began to make strong guaranteed income each month.

But that stress paid off. These days, I make more money blogging than I ever made in my old life.

5. If you had to do it all over again, what would you change?

There's not a lot I would have changed, but I would have implemented affiliates on my site earlier and I would have developed a product of my own at an earlier date. Though I've been so busy that I don't know how I ever would have found the time! Affiliates were a financial game-changer for me and I feel like I'm far behind the herd when it comes to having my own product. But I'm making up for both now.

6. Is there anything else you'd like to add based on your experience?

If you want to become a professional travel blogger, know what you're getting into. The vast majority of people never make enough money to live off it and the few who do only got to that point after years of often thankless work. It's much more difficult today than when I started nearly five years ago -- there's more competition and you're behind the 8-ball, so to speak. But that doesn't mean it's impossible.

CHAPTER 5

CREATING MONEY OFFLINE

I already went through an extensive list of ways in which you can create a micro-business and a living online. These are all worth trying at some point or another – depending on your interest. But I also want to cover a few methods in which you can make a living or generate some money offline, either before you leave or while you're location independent.

Before I dig in, I want to mention something very important. Offline businesses or moneymaking tactics are inherently attached to the location in which they are performed, so once you decide to move from one place to another, you'll either start from scratch or notice that the tactic might not translate as well to the new location.

When it comes to offline methods, I only recommend them to generate some extra income for a short period. It doesn't hurt to make some extra cash on the side, especially if it helps you reach a goal sooner, and you love doing that certain activity.

So, let's start with a few tactics you can do *before* you leave home:

BEFORE GETTING ON THE ROAD

Sales of Products

It is similar to the online sales of products, but here you are responsible for arranging the entire process in person, or at least most of it.

Do you have a talent or skills you can use to create something you can sell? This is one of the most basic ways to earn some sporadic extra income. Can you bake cakes and sell them? Buy something wholesale and sell them for a profit? This references back to the buy low, sell high technique detailed in the previous chapter, but in this case, you're doing everything offline.

Tap on any skills you have and do weekend sales in your community, weekly sales at work, or among friends. Craigslist can be a good place to start advertising your products around your neighborhood, and it is free! If Craigslist is not available or widely used in your country or city, Google search for sites that display local ads and try listing your products there. The point here is not to become an online business, but to reach more people in your community through online ads.

Sales of Services

Can you offer your services in your extra time for some extra money? Can you help paint or clean a house on the weekends? Again, you can use Craigslist or local ads site to offer your services.

There's also TaskRabbit.com, which helps you achieve this in a more organized environment. People can list their cleaning, handyman, personal assistance, and moving help services on their website, set their hourly rate, and the locations they can serve. Plus, you have the opportunity to earn tips is you do well your tasks.

I learned about TaskRabbit after a friend of mine tried the service for 28 days as an experiment. He did 31 tasks in that month, working tasks that ranged from 30 minutes to 6 hours, and made a total of $1760. That's no small change, especially if you're doing this on the side. Sure, my friend did it intensively since he wasn't working at the time, but in total, he earned more per hour than the average worker in the US.

Garage Sale (aka, get rid of everything)

This can help push up your savings a month or a few weeks before you leave. Get rid of absolutely everything you don't need for your location independent life or don't feel that is important to keep. You can sell them to friends, relatives, through eBay, Craigslist, and through garage sales.

Investments, High-Interest Rate Banking, and Assets

I think this is slightly off topic since making a living with investments and High-Interest Rates banking means you already have assets on your side, and this is not really "working for money." But still, I'll mention it as an option.

On a flight from Bangkok to Yangon, I met Monique, a Canadian lady in her 60s who has been traveling the world for at least 20 years now. I asked her, how do you manage to travel for so long? She manages to travel indefinitely thanks to the interest rates she earns on her savings (earned when she sold her house years ago). While I don't know exactly how much money she has, I'm pretty sure she has enough to allow her to offset her low budget travel expenses with her interest income.

Investment works the same (in general), but while investment can give greater returns, it can also be risky since investments can be lost or reduced if the market turns.

Finally, I know of travelers who manage to "earn an income" solely based on their home or property rental. While they travel, they rent their property either through long-term contracts or through AirBnb.com to cover the mortgage (if they still have it) and have a few extra dollars to travel. Nancy Vogel of FamilyonBikes.org is one of those, who currently funds her family's trips through real estate rentals.

WHILE ON THE ROAD

Teach English

Teaching English is one of the most common jobs travelers get while abroad.   It is fun, but it is also a lot of work. You might be required to have a bachelor degree, or depending on the country, you might need to certify yourself as a TESL teacher (Teaching English as a Second Language). Certain countries like Japan, South Korea, and China, among others, offer long-term positions for TESL certified travelers.

These countries I mentioned could be strict with the certification requirement since they have a high demand. They look for high-quality teachers, but in return they pay well (over $1,000 a month) and in many cases give good benefits – like paying for your accommodation in addition to your salary. But, should you be contracted, usually you have to stay in that one destination for the term of one year, renewable. Still, you can choose to explore the area or country more in depth during your time off. Should you find a teaching job before you leave, some of the most reputable schools in these countries might be able to pay for your flights from your home country, should they include that in your contract. But, this is often offered to people who already have experience as a TESL teacher.

Should you not want to certify yourself, you can get odd jobs teaching English for short terms, but these often pay less and might be located in less popular or developed places like Laos, Thailand, and Indonesia, among others. On the other hand, these less developed countries allow you to negotiate your contract better to have more flexibility to travel or for any specific duration.

Or, you could do like my friend Earl of WanderingEarl.com did. When he was in Chiang Mai, he created a few simple fliers offering his Conversational English lessons and pasted them around the university campus. After a few hours of placing the flyers, he had enough students calling him that he was able to set up two daily sessions of 5 students each, charging around $3 per student per session. It might not sound like enough money to you, but earning $30 to spend an hour or so (twice a day) chatting with students to help them learn English is more than enough money to live in Chiang Mai.

Should you not be a native English speaker, you could teach Spanish, German, Italian, French, or any other common language. You'd be surprised how demand varies per country.

In any of the cases mentioned above, you must be a "people person" to teach a language. Depending on the job you find, you might find yourself working 30 hours a week with kids from elementary to high school, plus tutoring (in some cases). It goes without saying that as a teacher, you must look professional, have good manners, and know how to respect the foreign culture.

I recommend reading through Audrey's post in ThatBackpacker.com to learn more about how she makes a living and travels the world teaching English (especially her post on teaching and living in South Korea).

How to Find a TESL Job

You can approach this in two ways; from home by searching online, or in person right after you arrive at your destination.

Searching from home is good if you know for sure where you're going and know that you want to teach during your trip or time settled in a new location. You can screen dozens of schools from home, interview with them, and negotiate your contract. You can have the comfort of knowing that once you arrive at your destination, you'll be taken care of by the school.

The downside of this approach is that you won't be able to inspect the school beforehand, so you don't know how your working environment looks. Should the school environment or teachers not be the most optimal for you (or even for the students) you will be stuck there for the duration of your contract.

On the other hand, should you want to search for schools in person after you reach your destination, you can visit them, inspect the facilities, meet the faculty and director, and possibly leverage your contract better since you know exactly what you're getting yourself into. Plus, you're negotiating face to face with the director, not a possible third party.

The following are some resources to search for TESL jobs:

- *JetProgramme.org* - A Japanese government-run program that places thousands of native English speakers in teaching positions throughout Japan. It is competitive, but they give generous salary and benefits.

- *ESLCafé.com* - A large and useful database of teaching positions around the world. (The site can be a bit messy, though)
- *GoAbroad.com* – Their Teach Abroad section is informative and useful for anyone interested in teaching English.
- *TEFL.net* – Information about Teaching English as a Foreign Language (TEFL) certification courses.
- *TEFL.com* – Another good resource for certification courses.

Working Holiday Visas

Working holiday visas are visas given specifically to 18 to 30 years old travelers who want to work for part of their time abroad. The idea behind a working holiday visa is to allow travelers to stay longer in a specific country to have an in-depth experience in it, live like a local, and make some money along the way. These often end up being life-changing experiences since you get to live in a completely different way and get to learn new customs.

While their duration ranges from three months to two years, the most common visas last one year. The duration also depends on which country you're from and to which country you're going.

The fact that the visa might last a year doesn't mean that you must stay in the country for that amount of time. But, it is often recommended to stay the entirety of the time allowed by the visa to take the most advantage of it.

Working holiday visas have to be applied for before arriving in the country to get stamped in by immigration through the working holiday scheme instead of the typical tourist visa.

Financially, some working holiday visas might be free while others cost a decent amount of money. For example, the Australian Working Holiday Visa costs AUD$420. But, even though you might have to pay for a visa, the advantage you have is that you can work legally for a limited time (from three months to a year or more) and earn that money back, and much more. You will still need to pay for your flights and accommodation, but again, depending on which country you go to, the money you earn will offset these costs.

In some cases, depending on the type of work you do, there's the possibility of getting sponsored by an employer, which will allow you to stay in the country for a much longer period.

Have in mind that not all nationalities are accepted for working holiday visas, so if you're interested in doing it, you should check your intended destination's immigration site to see if your nationality is on their acceptance list.

These are the most common destinations where working holiday visas are widely practiced:

Australia: They allow you to live in the country for up to a year, including the opportunity to study for up to four months or work for up to six months within that year. Should you decide to work on a farm, you'll have better chances of earning a better salary (those are the best-paid jobs there for working holiday visas) and have the opportunity to extend your visa for a second year. The

12-month duration of the visas starts the day you enter the country, not when you apply for it. You must be 30 or under to apply for it.

For more information and to apply, go to http://www.immi.gov.au/.

Canada: Their SWAP program allows students (or recent students) the opportunity to live and work in Canada for up to six months. The organization that runs this program is called BUNAC, and you can learn more about them or apply here: http://www.bunac.org/

France: The working holiday experience in France could be a bit of a challenge if you don't know French, or it might be exactly what you're looking for if you want to learn French along the way. The program is only open during the summer and lasts three months. Language courses and homestays are also available through the global contact for the scheme, BUNAC: http://www.bunac.org/

Ireland: It offers a 12-month working holiday visa that is quite attractive and easy to get. You can apply for it up to 12 months after your most recent full-time university study. You'll need to show proof of university study and enough money to cover your expenses during your stay (at least for the beginning). For more information and to apply, go to http://www.dfa.ie/.

New Zealand: They allow you to apply for the working holiday visa as long as you're 30 or under. They also have one of the greatest selection of nationalities they allow to apply, and depending on your nationality, the visa might be free (US citizens get it free). While it is similar to the Australian visa, you might also need to provide proof that you have enough money to sustain yourself while in the country, and in some cases, proof of an onward ticket out of the country too. For more information and to apply, head to http://www.immigration.govt.nz/.

Singapore: While they only allow citizens from some first world countries to apply for it (Australia, France, Germany, Hong Kong, Japan, New Zealand, UK, and the US), the Singaporean Working Holiday Pass Program allows anyone between the age of 17-30 and are either undergraduate students or have graduated from a university to work on any type of job for up to 6 months. To learn more and to apply, go to http://www.mom.gov.sg/

Lastly, some countries limit the amount of working holiday visas they give to foreigners from certain countries on a yearly basis. If you're interested in doing this, check all the information and requirements with enough time to make sure you can apply for it when you intend to travel.

Some additional resources to help you find jobs overseas:

- *Jobaroo.com* – Temporary and seasonal job opportunities in Australia.
- *SeasonalJobs.co.nz* – Temporary and seasonal job opportunities in New Zealand.
- *AnyworkAnywhere.com* – A database of temporary jobs in the UK and worldwide.
- *JobMonkey.com* – A job database with permanent, seasonal, and temporary jobs around the world.

- *SeasonWorkers.com* – Seasonal work opportunities around the world.
- *GapWork.com* – Another short-term jobs database.

"Under the table" Jobs

Technically this is not legal, but hey, in the real world there are a lot of gray areas, especially when you're traveling. I want to note that should you pursue anything listed here; it will be at your own risk.

Under the table jobs are those small or unofficial jobs you find on the street or by meeting people randomly. They tend to pay you cash or pay just enough so that they don't have to report it to their local treasury department.

In general, you won't make much money, but chances are that you won't be spending much money at the same time either. And, nothing beats earning some cash instead of nothing!

Jobs can range from a few days to a few weeks or months, depending on what you find. The easiest ones you can find are the ones in which you exchange a few hours of daily work at a hostel for room and board (food and a bed). You might be doing anything from cleaning, to attending guests, to doing maintenance. In some cases, should you decide to stay there longer, they might pay you some money for your work too.

Other easy to find jobs that pay under the table are manual jobs like farming, bartending, manual labor, construction, babysitting, and coffee shop work, among others. The food and beverage and the manual labor industry are often the most open to these arrangements. Among the jobs mentioned on the list, construction tends to be one of the highest paid since it is hard work and sometimes specialized.

How do you find these jobs?

Just ask around. You will not see official postings looking for "under the table" employees, but sometimes, when you see "worker needed" posts, you can just ask and present yourself as a long term traveler looking for work. Depending on how open the employer is to the idea, they might offer something to you, or simply tell you that's not possible.

Should you be really into a café that you visit often or any store in specific, you can ask politely if there's any "off the books" work available after they get to know who you are (a returning customer) – just enough for them to know you go there and enjoy the place.

Hostels are also great places to look for random jobs. Check their bulletin board, if they have one, or ask at the reception. Other travelers are also a great source of information.

The following are a few online resources where you could find a job:

- *LonelyPlanet.com* – Search their active Thorn Tree forum for any posting regarding jobs in your destination.
- *Bootsnall.com* – You can ask other travelers about unofficial works on their boards.

- *AnyworkAnywhere.com* – Sometimes they list an under the table job here and there.

Specialized Instructor

Do you have a special talent or knowledge you can teach? A lot of travelers use their talents to their advantage to earn some money, by teaching others the techniques to perform well in a specialized field. This can be teaching how to play an instrument, a sport, improve in fashion, magic, poker, etc.

Depending on the skills you have, you can either go through the working holiday visa path or the under the table path. For example, should you be a good dancer, you could work as a choreographer in a dance school. Probably, you might need a working holiday visa for that (if the country allows it), but chances are that in less developed countries you could just swing by a dance studio, show your talent, and maybe ask for a few hours of work.

The process of getting a job would follow the ones previously discussed on the working holiday visa section and the under the table section.

Be a Crewmember

There are two kinds of ships you can be a crewmember of: Cruise ships and sailboats/yacht.

Let's start with the sailboats and yacht – those "little" boats that go from 20 to a couple hundred feet long.

As fancy as it may sound, traveling and working on a sailboat or yacht is hard work. But, you'll have the advantage if you've sailed before, know your way around a boat, don't tend to get sea sick, and are used to live in tight quarters.

To do this, you must love spending days out on the sea, but still, this is a unique and adventurous way to travel the world.

If you don't have experience working on a boat, chances are that as a first timer, you won't get paid, unless they really need someone. But, if you're up for the experience, most novice crews get their accommodation and transportation for free (which is technically the boat trip), and in some cases, even the food. But hey, this is a great way to start traveling for free, or at least very cheap! For your first experience, I also recommend you do a short trip, so you see if life at the sea is really for you.

Would they hire you without experience? Sure, some captains are looking more for high-spirited, responsible, and sociable people to share the journey and the costs with. But, if you get hired, put yourself slightly ahead of the curve by doing a bit of research to get familiar with general nautical terms and some of the major safety procedures.

If you're experienced, then you could get a proper job on their crew for a specific journey that could take a few weeks or more, or for a longer period – like, crossing from South America to Europe, stopping in several ports along the way.

How to get a job on a boat?

As a rule of thumb, the bigger the boat, the more people the captain needs to sail it. And, even small boats need a few people since sailing is a 24 hours job, especially if you're deep in the sea. Or, sometimes it could be the wish of a couple to take a trip on their yacht and not have to work on their trip, so they would rely on you and others in the crew to take them wherever they want.

You can go to your local marina and search for crew openings there. Ask around, see if there are signs posted looking for crew, or, you could even advertise yourself as looking for a position and leave your flyer there. Or, if you don't have a decent marina close to you, you can fly to any tropical location with busy marinas since they will increase your chances of finding a crew position.

As mention before, some captains will be willing to cover all, if not most of your expenses, while others might want you to pay for your share of fuel, food, and mooring fees. Also, how much you get paid and how much you pay in fees and other expenses is highly dependent on the kind of trip you do and what you negotiate with the captain. In many cases you might not make a lot of money, or nothing at all after deducting your fees, but you still get to travel the world as an adventurer and get to visit some exotic locations that would cost a lot of money to fly to!

Depending on the size of the boat, crewmembers can work as mechanics, deckhand, cooks, cleaners, bartenders, electricians, and more. And yes, when it is time to work, boats demand a lot of work, so you might spend hours cleaning, repairing, and sailing.

Another tip to find a position is to visit the sailors' bars by the marina, have a few drinks and network there with other sailors. This is the one of the best ways to get a position since you're interacting with them socially, so they see who you are as a person, beyond your skills (or lack of them).

Recording your experience

You should create your "sailing resume" where you list your previous experiences and skills, from anything mechanical, to technical, and even any kind of entertainment you might know how to do. Also keep a log book with details of each voyage you took, on which kind of vessel, and how you participated on each of them, among other experiences. This, along with positive references is your best weapon to get a good job sailing the world and with good pay.

For more information about getting a job as a crewmember on a boat, you can check these sites:

- *SailNet.com*
- *CruisingWorld.com*
- *FindACrew.net*
- *FloatPlan.com*
- *SFSailing.com*
- *SpinSheet.com*
- *SouthWindsSailing.com*

Now, how do you work on a cruise?

Different from a sailboat or a yacht, working on a cruise is a more serious job where you will be contracted per seasons and work directly or indirectly with customers.

Cruises are famous for their camaraderie, not only among passengers but also among the crew, so you must be a high-spirited and energetic person to work on a cruise.

One of the biggest plus about working on a cruise is that most, if not all, of your expenses are covered since you're pretty much living in the cruise (your work environment) and the pay is quite good, so you'll be able to save more money than ever. Also, you get to travel to different countries on a weekly basis.

On the downside, you must get used to living in small quarters and be sure you're up for life at sea, which isn't necessarily for everyone.

Usually, contracts range from 4 to 8 months, depending on your position and the cruise you're in. Once you're contracted, the cruise company often covers your flights to the port of call and hotel, and all of them cover your uniforms, medical insurance, meals, and accommodation on the cruise. This means you have no expenses for the duration of your work.

But make no mistake, working on a cruise is hard work and often requires long working days. In many cases, there are none or few vacation days during your contract time, but once your contract is done, your next contract (should you decide to renew) starts after a few months of vacation in between.

Working on a cruise is more specialized than on a small boat since the crew is much bigger. On a cruise, you could dedicate to entertainment, the kitchen, cleaning, management, spas, retail, or other positions.

Also, depending on your position and experience, you might get to have your own cabin, or you might have to share with one or three more coworkers. For sure, you will need to be a sociable person since not only you'll have to interact with your coworkers almost 24/7, but also with the customers on board – from day one until the last day of your contract.

But, don't worry, not everything is work. Every couple weeks there are crew parties and during your time off you can relax in crew designated areas that share similar amenities as the passenger amenities – like spas, pools, entertainment areas, and so on.

If you don't have to work while the boat is on port, you have the opportunity to explore some of the greatest and exotic destinations from around the world, one port at a time.

Some resources you can use to look for a job on a cruise are:

- *AllCruiseJobs.com*
- *CruiseShipJobs.com*
- *Princess.com*
- *RoyalCaribbean.com*
- *Carnival.com*

To learn more about working on a cruise and how to apply for jobs as a crewmember, I recommend reading Wandering Earl's *How To Work On A Cruise Ship* guide since he worked as crew for several years and made a great living through it.

All these jobs listed before are just a few options of what you could do to make a living offline while traveling the world or settling in different places. There are hundreds of other options like acting as a Bollywood extra, translating documents and restaurant menus, being a tour guide, and so on. While they might work for you, most of these other options are just good enough to earn a few extra dollars, not to really make a living out of them in the long term.

If you're really looking for a location independent life, I recommend you focus on the online alternatives since they have more potential to free you from any specific location, and the income potential can vary greatly, giving returns of six figures a year and more in some cases.

Do not be embarrassed by your failures, learn from them and start again.
— RICHARD BRANSON

IN THEIR OWN WORDS

DEREK EARL BARON

Originally from: United States

Website: WanderingEarl.com and Plansify.com

1. What did you do before traveling (particularly to make a living) and what made you decide to become location independent?

I actually started traveling shortly after graduating from university, so I hadn't done anything yet in terms of making a living. I had worked odd jobs here and there throughout school to make some spending money but that was it. Once I graduated with my degree, my plan was simple - take off and travel for three months to SE Asia and then, once that trip was over, return home and begin my career as a sports agent.

And it was during the first couple of weeks of my trip to SE Asia that I realized traveling was far more rewarding that I had ever imagined and suddenly, I had this intense urge to find ways to keep on traveling for as long as I could. It all had to do with one thing - meeting so many new people from all over the planet, talking with them, learning from them and gaining such a wider view on life and on the world. This one aspect of travel is what convinced me to give up my career goals and try to focus on creating a life of travel instead.

2. How did you deal with different aspects of becoming location independent? (emotionally, socially, and financially)

At first, I wasn't location independent. I taught English in Thailand and then worked as a Tour Manager on board cruise ships on and off for several years. It wasn't until 2008 that I first began working online and truly being able to work from anywhere.

For me, it was an ideal setup from the start. I had found ways to earn an income while being able to continue traveling or living almost anywhere I wanted. So it was an easy lifestyle for me to adjust to. Financially, things started off slow, as I had expected of course, and that's how I quickly realized that I had to organize my location independent lifestyle in order to succeed. I knew that if I continued bouncing around the world at my usual pace, I would never be able to concentrate enough on my work for it to actually become fully sustainable long-term. So I changed up my life a bit and started having a 'base'. For example, I stayed in Mexico for 2 years, coming and going often, but always having that familiar place to return to. After Mexico, I started using Romania as my base, again, coming and going all the time, but having that familiar place to come back to whenever I needed to buckle down and really get some work done. This helped me get into a routine that allowed me to make real progress with the projects I've worked on.

This set up also helped me in terms of my social life. For years I had gotten used to saying hello and goodbye to all of the wonderful people I met during my travels and never knowing when or if I would see them again. But by having a base to return to, I also had a group of friends that I returned to as well. And having those friends in Mexico and Romania made the adjustment to this lifestyle even easier. Right now, whenever I arrive back in Romania, just like that I have a familiar bed, a familiar handful of cafes to work from and a familiar group of friends to hang out with again. It's as if I have the benefits of a 'home' and 'hometown' without actually having a home.

In my case, I now know that had I not made these adjustments and organized my life around a base, I would not have been able to carry on with this lifestyle for too long.

3. What prompted you to choose this specific path of income and how did your previous job help you get there?

While on board one of the cruise ships I used to work on, a friend and fellow crew member once suggested that I try 'working online', maybe writing an eBook based on all my travel knowledge. So I did. And it worked. About a year later, after I had given up my cruise ship career, I was with that same friend in a small town in Mexico. One day, he told me he read a book about the growing popularity of blogs and he thought I should start a travel blog. I read a little about what a travel blog was exactly and then I started one. And again, it worked. Of course, it was a long, challenging journey, but as soon as I saw the first comment on my blog from someone who was not a friend or family member, I realized that this blogging stuff could actually turn into something that might allow me to continue being location independent for a long time. From there, I've just listened. I've listened to what my readers ask, what they want to learn and how they want to learn it. I then work on projects aimed at providing exactly what they want, and that's how I've ended up writing eBooks, organizing and leading small-group tours around the world and creating my new travel startup, Plansify.com

4. How do you evaluate your current situation (financially and emotionally) compared to your "past life"?

In my situation, my past life was simply my early travel years, before I started working online. And while I loved absolutely every minute (okay, most minutes) of those earlier experiences, I am definitely more comfortable with my current situation. I think it also has to do with age. As you get older, you want a little more comfort and security and you don't want to continue scrapping and clawing to get just enough to survive. Right now, things are rolling along, I'm working on new projects all the time and my blog continues to grow. Each year my situation is getting better and better and the hard work is paying off. And while I do work more now than ever before, I enjoy the work I do and that makes a major difference. In the end, it's all about paying attention to yourself and making adjustments. Just because you love one form of travel one day, doesn't mean you'll love it the next. Your needs and desires change over time and you must make changes to your life when it happens in order to ensure that you remain happy with your situation and living the life you really want to be living.

5. If you had to do it all over again, what would you change?

The only thing I would change would be taking this lifestyle a little more seriously from the start. Instead of just bouncing around the world without much of a purpose for those first handful of years, I realize now that I could have focused on a particular goal or tried to turn those experiences and the knowledge I was gaining into something more substantial at the time. This would have helped me create a stronger foundation early on and in turn, give my life a little more direction from an early stage. It took many years for me to truly figure out how to become location independent because I got such a late start with trying to focus on making that happen.

6. Is there anything else you'd like to add based on your experience?

Location independence comes in infinite forms. I think many people get caught up in thinking that it means one thing - working online and traveling from place to place all the time. But that's just one form and there are thousands of people out there in the world who have found their own unique way to make this lifestyle a reality. Yes, you can work online and travel around at the same time. You could also travel slowly and stay in each destination for 1 month or 3 months or even 1 year before moving on. You could work half the year from one destination and travel to other countries during the other half. You don't even have to travel! You could stay in your home country and still be location independent. Maybe you want to travel for 2 months of the year and stay at home the rest. That works too! The important thing to remember is that there is no 'right' way to create this lifestyle.

The only 'right' way is the way that works for you and brings you the most happiness.

CHAPTER 6

SAVING MONEY

As obvious as it might sound, personal finance is personal, so just as you took control and determined your life and business goals, you should also manage your financial priorities to help you achieve those goals.

SETTING A METRIC

Setting a continual metric can help you stay focused on what you want to achieve. We already discussed goal setting in Chapter 2, so now we must apply the same ideas to our financial goals.

We must start by establishing a financial priority that goes along, or at least reflects the intentions behind our other goals. I can't tell you a specific saving amount since it all depends on what you can afford to save and how much are you prioritizing financially that goal you have in mind. But know this, if part of your goal is to travel to a dream destination, even saving $2 a day will take you there in a matter of a few years or less.

If your financial goal is business oriented, then how much money does your business idea requires? As I mentioned before, starting a business does not necessarily require a high financial investment, so it's probable your business idea can become a reality much sooner than you think.

When you're preparing to get on the road, saving money is crucial not only to be able to pay for all the experiences we want, but also to have some reserve money in case our business takes longer than expected to take off or has a few rough months.

Now, how do you save all that money?

I can't tell you of exact ways to manage your money since this will vary drastically, but I can at least tell you what I did to save money for my round the world trip. The following are 20 ways I used to grow my travel fund an average of $1,000 per month before I started my trip.

1. Dedicate a separate savings account for your travel fund – This account is your focus. This will be the measure of your progress towards your ultimate goal: reaching your travel budget and taking off on that long-term trip or location independent lifestyle! You should think of that money as "non-existent" so that you won't count on it for anything until you leave for your trip.

2. Track your expenses – Use a budgeting tool like Mint.com to track all your expenses and see where your money is going. This will help you know what expenses can be cut and how much could you invest in your trip. Mint is very user-friendly and a valuable tool when it comes to budgeting.

3. Pay yourself first – Once you know how much you can dedicate per month to your travel budget, make it an automatic transfer to your "travel fund" account the exact day you receive your paycheck. That way you won't be tempted to spend it unnecessarily. A way to save for travel is making it a priority.

4. Do small weekly transfers – In addition to your automatic monthly transfer, do small weekly transfers that won't feel hard in your pocket. For example, every week I transfer $20 to my travel fund, in addition to the monthly saving amount. Those $20s have gone a long way on my savings!

5. Reduce your housing expenses – If possible, move to a cheaper apartment or consider getting roommates. When I was saving for my trip, I moved from an amazing studio to living with roommates. That move alone added more than $400 per month to my travel fund.

6. Reduce your utility bills – Not only reducing your electricity, water, and gas bills are good for the environment, but it will add a few dollars to your funds.

7. Quit or reduce smoking – While I don't smoke, I know of people who spend around $300 in cigarettes per month. Imagine if you could cut that at least in half!

8. Starbucks? – Again, I don't drink coffee... but, what if you could reduce your $4 lattes per day consumption?

9. Take your lunch to work or take advantage of lunch specials – I admit I didn't take my lunch to work too often, but I took advantage of cheap street cart food, value menus, and lunch specials.

10. Netflix a movie instead of going out to the movie theater – Go to Netflix.com or Hulu.com (The US only) to watch your favorite movies or TV shows. The price difference is insane, especially if movie tickets cost $13, as in New York.

11. Cut out cable TV – I lived without cable for over two years and still was able to watch all my favorite shows online on each network's website, or just watched Netflix. Also, several TV stations allow you to stream their popular shows online on their website. This alone helped me save over $60 per month.

12. Clean out your credit – If you have debt, pay first your credit cards with the highest interest. After that one is fully paid, add that payment amount to the card with the next highest interest rate. Eventually, you will snowball your debt to zero! Also, get a credit card with a year or more of 0% interest and transfer your balance. Chances are that the 3% transfer fee is much less than the total interest that would be paid for the life of the debt.

13. Do social buying and coupons – Clipping coupons is nothing to be embarrassed about. On today's market, social buying and coupon sites like Groupon.com have helped millions of people buy what they need for much less than the retail price. Just be careful not to buy stuff you don't need just because they are cheap.

14. Use public transportation – If you live in a city with a decent public transportation and it is accessible to you, consider using it instead of using your car all the time. Not only could you save money, but it's also environmentally friendly.

15. Save money on your actual travel planning – Piling up the money is half the story on staying long term on the road. Saving on your travel expenses is the other half. Compare prices on various sites and try different travel combinations to see which one is cheaper or brings "more bang for your buck". Becoming a travel hacker is an art form in itself that will help you save hundreds, if not thousands, of dollars on your trip. Flexibility is the key! I talk more about travel hacking later in the guide.

16. Don't overlook free events – Many cities have free festivals, concerts, and other events that are as good as many paid events, especially during the summer months.

17. Cancel your Gym – Be creative with your physical training by jogging around the city, exercising at the park, or going to free public "exercise parks" available in most cities. It's a good way to burn the calories without burning your cash.

18. Change your phone plan – If you're not using all your minutes or features included in your phone plan, consider changing it to a cheaper one. In my case, I changed the plan I had for three years with limited minutes, unlimited text and web for $70, to an all unlimited prepaid plan for $50. I had more minutes and was saving $20 per month!

19. Take a second job or freelance – We went over this already in the "create money" section. If you have an expertise you think you can offer, present yourself as a freelancer for some extra income. If you blog and can monetize it, that's a big step too since it could help you extend your trip by still earning some money while on the road.

20. Sell your stuff – If you're getting rid of your apartment, maybe it's wise to sell some of your possessions instead of spending more money on storage. Either do a garage sale or post you things on eBay or Craigslist to reach a wider market. This alone can give a big push to your savings at the last stage of your planning.

By putting into action all these techniques I was able to save around $1,000 per month. Depending on your case and income level you might be able to save less, or save much more. But even if it's just a small amount that you're saving per month, the important thing is to have a goal in mind and keep your focus on achieving it at an established date in the future. That way you will keep your drive and get to realize your location independent lifestyle sooner rather than later!

You don't choose the day you enter the world and you don't chose the day you leave. It's what you do in between that makes all the difference.
– ANITA SEPTIMUS

FRUGALITY AND SPENDING

Since I prioritized my goals in life, I became a frugal person. But, I don't practice frugality just to pinch on every penny I can, I practice it to choose consciously the things I value and truly need. So, what do I value? I value life experiences over material possessions. Having said that, this doesn't mean you should value life experiences the same way I do, after all, it is your life and money. So, what do you value?

Years ago before I started traveling, I probably went shopping for a new t-shirt or pants every month or so. That was fine, as I didn't have any financial priority at the moment. Now, I barely buy new clothes once or twice a year, when I truly feel like I need them. Why? Now I'm more conscious of my spending.

Yesterday I was at the mall and saw this cool t-shirt I wanted to buy. For a while, I got tempted into buying it, but after some thought I convinced myself that I didn't need it. I also practiced this one trick I imposed on myself when I started saving money to travel. I had $100 cash at home for any random purchase, so whenever I went shopping and saw something I didn't really need but really liked, I forced myself not to buy it at the moment and only buy it with the $100 I had in my apartment. This was an auto-imposed hoop for me to think about that purchase. If I really wanted to buy it, I had to go home, pick the $100 (or whatever amount it costs), and go back to the store to purchase it. More often than not, I ended convincing myself on the way that I didn't need it, thus saving my money in the end.

Neat trick, eh? Why don't you practice it too? Why don't you think of other ways to auto-impose hoops that will make you more conscious of your spending?

Another trick I use often is correlating spending values. For example, I might like to buy a new backpack, but do I need a new backpack? If I don't because I know my current backpack still works, then I start correlating prices with travel experiences. For example, this $100 backpack is equal to what I would spend in 4 days in Thailand, or 2 dives in the Maldives, or a week in India, and so on. This often helps me prioritize on the experiences.

In the end, I recommend you to do what you think works best for you and prioritize on what you believe will bring the most value to your life.

People will always try to stop you from doing the right thing if it is unconventional.
– WARREN BUFFETT

IN THEIR OWN WORDS

GUSTAVO JUNQUEIRA

Originally from: Brazil

Website: Vagamundagem.com

1. What did you do before traveling (particularly to make a living) and what made you decide to become location independent?

I was a student of Aeronautical Engineering. I dropped out to become a pilot opening my way of becoming location independent, until I realized that I did not need to be a pilot or have a boss to travel the world non-stop.

My income to start traveling non-stop came from selling chocolate bonbons at school, working in an insurance office during high school, and also from building airplanes in my university (with a scholarship).

2. How did you deal with different aspects of becoming location independent? (emotionally, socially, and financially)

I started traveling a lot when I got into university and I spent all my holidays and vacations traveling abroad, especially to work in the USA. Even if I had 5 days without class I would find a way to go to USA and paint a house, for example. It was not for the money but to fulfill my desire of traveling. When the opportunity came to become location independent I was more than ready. There are off course some difficulties dealing with missing family and friends, but I got used to it and I try to keep in constant communication with people I love back home.

I need to confess though that finance is a constant concern because I do not have a business that brings me lots of money. I do much more to save money than to make it, but I think I need to have the attitude and face the unknown and the so-called "instability" to go for my dream of travel the world. Slowly the big puzzle of how I could keep doing that forever came in place and even though I am still not making the amount I would think is comfortable, the unforgettable experiences that are following my decision are the proof that I should not worry too much about it!

3. What prompted you to choose this specific path of income and how did your previous job help you get there?

The job that most helped me to get where I am today is the one that has nothing to do with what I do. I used to work in an office selling insurance, sitting in a chair in a stall, between 4 walls as many people in the world do and just how most of the engineers (my would-be future profession) work today. I was absolutely sure that I did not want to work or spend my life in that way and going away from what others thought I should do seemed the right way to go!

I do many things to keep my status as independent location, from flying airplanes to cleaning houses, to managing vacation rental houses through the internet and currently investing in the knowledge of travel writing and online entrepreneurship.

4. How do you evaluate your current situation (financially and emotionally) compared to your "past life"?

I have a peace of mind now to know I am living my biggest dream. The one I used to think I would just achieve when I retired. That peace of mind of doing what you love overcomes any financial concerns I face every now and then.

Finding ways to support this way of living makes it easy to keep this path. And there are plenty of them nowadays! You just need to conciliate what you like doing with your dream of traveling. It might not be easy but is for sure rewarding!

My only concern is to keep my biggest dream of traveling alive before I drown with so many options of making money popping up every day in my laptop screen. Meeting people, keep traveling and living simple should not give way to make more money in my view. I do not like the idea of disguising the will of making money with a freedom lifestyle. You can keep traveling forever but if you cannot stop thinking in how to make more money, the "freedom" is only an illusion.

5. If you had to do it all over again, what would you change?

I would have dropped out from university earlier!

6. Is there anything else you'd like to add based on your experience?

To become location independent can be overwhelming and you might not be sure how to start and how you can keep your status as really "independent". Don't worry too much about it. Most of the location independent friends I have started traveling not really knowing they would become one. If you still are not sure what you can do to finance this lifestyle, save a little bit and go traveling for a few months so you can have time to make sure you enjoy the life on the road and also for some reflection that will hopefully lead to a way of making a living while traveling. While you travel make sure you learn ways to save money and to appreciate traveling and living in a simple way. That way you do not need to spend so much time and energy making money itself!

CHAPTER 7

TRAVELING WITH DEBT

This section is not written to encourage you to travel with debt, but to help you understand that it is possible to travel even if you have debt. The trick lies in knowing how to control and pay off that debt before traveling or even while you're traveling long term.

According to debt.org, on average, each household in the US with a credit card carries more than $15,000 in credit card debt. That doesn't count student loan debt, which is also common in the US and often much higher than credit card debt.

Debt is one of the most common deterrents when it comes to travel, and it is understandable since you have to handle the debt you carry. But, should debt keep you from traveling or becoming location independent?

Let's put this scenario. Let's say you don't want to travel because you have debt, and you would feel irresponsible if you traveled with debt. I'll say that you have just $4,000 in credit card debt and only pay the minimum monthly payments (and have an APR of 15.99%). Did you know that it would take you over 11 years to pay that debt? Sure, you can pay more per month to bring the debt down much faster –like $70 a month to pay it in 3 years– but, you see what I mean; debt can take a long time to pay.

And then there are the student loans, which are scheduled to be paid in 10, 15, 20, or 30 years depending on your loan.

Would you really want to delay your dreams for that long?

I believe you shouldn't, but at the same time, I believe you should prepare properly (or I should say, even better) to enter this "lifestyle" if you have debt.

When I started traveling I had credit card debt and throughout the trip I've paid it, accumulated some again, and paid it again. It happens. But, I've handled whatever debt I had and prepared my finances to pay them every single month, no matter where I am or how I feel financially.

Before leaving NYC, I left with the hopes of traveling the world for one year with the $18,000 I had in my bank account at that time. That amount of money is enough to travel for a year (as I'll show you later in this guide), but the truth is that those $18K were not all for travel. About 1/3 of that money was *exclusively* saved to pay my student loans for a year plus a few months, as well as my credit cards.

If I had the money from the beginning, why not pay the credit card and travel without that debt? Sure, I could have done it and honestly, I would have saved some money by avoiding the interest charges on my account. But, I preferred to have some money I could count on in the long run in case something happened or for any emergency. I wasn't used to long term travel, so I didn't know how I would react financially to it. At the time, the blog was already generating some money, so I tried my best to use that income to offset some of that debt.

MANAGING YOUR DEBT ON THE ROAD

Now, should you decide to travel or become location independent with a current debt, these are the things you should do.

DISCLAIMER: I am not a financial planner or accountant. These are only recommendations I'm giving based on my experience and what worked for me. Should you have serious financial problems, you should consult with a professional.

Create a debt management plan that will tackle the following:

1. Decide which credit cards will be paid off first.

You must dig into your accounts and see these two main factors:

What interest rates are you paying, and which card has the highest?

What are your current balances, and which card has the lowest?

Each case will be different, but optimally you will want to pay off first the credit card with the highest interest rate. But sometimes, paying off the card with the smallest balance feels so good since it will make you feel less overwhelmed. It is like a small win in your quest to be debt free. Still, I recommend paying off first (or at least giving the highest payment) to the card with the highest interest rate. The less interest you pay, in the long run, the more you save and the quicker you get out of debt.

2. Practice the Snowball effect

Once you pay off one credit card, whatever amount of money you used to pay to that one card, apply it to the rest, so the other cards receive a higher payment per month. In theory, while you have less debt, you should still pay the same amount as before, or more, to reduce the amount of interest you pay and get rid of that debt faster.

3. Pay more than the minimum

Paying the minimum is no way to get out of debt. You should pay twice or more the minimum per card (if possible) to make a real impact on your credit card balance.

4. Eliminate Service Charges

Some banks charge a monthly fee to "maintain" your account or to do certain transactions; others don't. Check how much are you paying in banking fees, and if it is a decent amount, check for other banking option in which you will pay less, or preferably, none.

5. Have a strong will on future credit card purchases

If you still need to use your credit card, promise yourself that you will use it on things that you know you're capable of paying full by the end of the current billing cycle. In practice, these new purchases you make will not be added to your debt since you will be paying it full before the current cycle ends.

6. Reduce your spending

Make sure that from now on you spend much less than what you earn to not only reduce your debt but also to be able to save money and increase your reserve.

7. Search for cards with better or 0% introductory interest rates to transfer your balance

Now and then I see excellent credit card options with no interest rates for a year or more. The idea is to transfer your current balance to these cards so you can have an X amount of months without paying interest rates to pay off your debt faster. Have in mind, though, that balance transfers often charge 3% of the balance to be transferred, so take that fee into account when you calculate the possible savings of a 0% introductory interest rate card.

8. Consolidate your debt

Sometimes it is better to consolidate a bunch of smaller debts into a single debt through a consolidation loan or balance transfers. The point is to consolidate at a lower interest rate so you can take advantage of that interest saving. Trust me, consolidating a bunch of credit cards with 15%+ interest rate to a single card with 0% or a loan with 7% percent makes a huge difference. Consolidation loans can be acquired through local banks, but more often than not, you can get lower interest rates with crowdfunded loans through platforms like LendingClub.com and LendingTree.com. I got a Lending Club loan while in NYC, and even with their origination fee, I managed to save a lot of money in the long run due to the low interest rate. How can they give such low rates? Basically, instead of a bank lending you the money, a lot of people fund your loan, so when you make your monthly payments, you're actually paying back your "backers."

Look also into consolidating your student loans to have a single payment, which often can be lower than all your student loan payments combined.

9. Look for interest relief on your student loans

If you can't consolidate your student loans, you can search for government-sponsored interest relief programs. Some of these programs require you to spend a few weeks tutoring children or other voluntary work to qualify for their interest relief or debt reduction benefit. Google search for student loan relief programs or visit the financial aid office of your alma mater to ask about any current programs.

What I did...

I pretty much followed all these steps I just mentioned. When I was in NYC, I had three credit cards with a decent balance in them ($10,000+). I decided to pay $600 per month within all three (which was much more than the minimum). Once one card was paid off, I continued paying that total amount within the other two and so on. I also did the balance transfer option, since, for me, one year of 0% outweighed the 3% fee of the transfer.

I still left NYC with some debt (including my student loans), so if like me, you decide to travel with debt, you should still do the steps mentioned above, plus have a debt contingency.

Before leaving home for good, make sure you have saved enough money to cover your monthly payments for the amount of time you plan to travel or be location independent. You should also plan for a few extra months as a contingency plan when you come back home (if that's your case).

This works well if your debt is too big to pay off in a matter of a few months. If you can pay it in just a few months, you can either decide to wait a bit to start your trip debt free, or still start your trip but have that money saved to manage your debt responsibility.

Even though you might expect to make money on the way and use it to live and pay off your debt, I still recommend having the full amount (or at least a high portion) to cover your debt for the duration of your trip since you never know what could happen on the road. One month you might do well, but the next month you might make $0 out of your business or work.

After you're done paying them, should you still use credit cards?

I encourage using credit cards for their convenience, but only after you understand how to manage your spending and try to pay off the balance each month.

Not only credit cards are convenient for payments, but they are also excellent for travel hacking, which I'll explain further in Chapter 9.

Finally, if you're in debt and looking for a way out of it, know that you're not alone. There are thousands of blogs out there that share tips and strategies to manage debt and get rid of it as quick as possible. I recommend GetRichSlowly.org and ManVsDebt.com.

———

To help you keep track of the financial aspects of planning a trip and understanding your current financial situation, I've added some bonus worksheets available to you through this link: http://www.globotreks.com/worksheets/

———

Stop worrying about the potholes in the road and celebrate the journey.
– FITZHUGH MULLAN

———

IN THEIR OWN WORDS

CAZ & CRAIG MAKEPEACE

Originally from: Australia

Website: yTravelBlog.com

1. What did you do before traveling (particularly to make a living) and what made you decide to become location independent?

I was a primary (elementary) school teacher and Craig played professional rugby league and then became a carpenter. We kind of were location independent with those careers. By this I mean, we used these portable jobs as a way to live in other countries.

We'd work and travel that region for a couple of years, save money and set off for a longer travel experience in between relocations. We loved that travel lifestyle that much that we decided to pursue our own business so we would have more freedom and not have to rely on jobs and visas.

2. How did you deal with different aspects of becoming location independent? (emotionally, socially, and financially)

I always have a back up plan in place before I leave. This helps me to feel safe and to walk forward with more enthusiasm and hope than fear. If you don't calm your fears down before you leave then the chances of you quitting are a lot higher.

I think about what the worst possible scenario would be and create a plan for that. So for this Australian road trip, I realized that if we failed and ran out of money, I could always come home and live with my in-laws again and work at a supermarket. I knew I wasn't going to die. That was the absolute worst and I was okay with that.

Once I was okay with that, I knew the risk was worth it. How did I know? I simply thought of what the best case scenario would be and then acted towards that.

We've now been on the road for 16 months, our business has more than doubled in growth, the opportunities presented to us are huge and life couldn't be better. No scanning groceries in sight.

Maintaining my health is a huge part of dealing with being location independent. It can be exhausting work so it's important to look after your body. I eat a nutritious diet (most of the time) I meditate daily and I try to do yoga every day. We spent a lot of time outdoors, which I think elevates my energy and makes me feel calm.

At the moment, we are on the move a lot and being in our own country, we have a few friends scattered around the country and we have met so many people travelling. So the social side of things never seem to be a problem. We always make an effort to meet local people, whether that is through meet up groups, or just simply chatting to people we meet on the street. And the girls are so great at making friends, they are playing with someone new every day almost.

To manage financially, we just need to ensure we are still creating and producing so the income is flowing in. We sometimes have to stop in a places for a few weeks at a time to catch up on work. It is so challenging when you have kids. We hope to have a better system in place before we attempt our next adventure together.

3. What prompted you to choose this specific path of income and how did your previous job help you get there?

I always loved writing, but never believed I wrote something anyone would care to read. Craig always loved taking photos so when we discovered travel blogs, it felt like an easy path for us to walk down. We had travelled around the world for about 10 years before we started so we knew we had a wealth of stories and tips we could share to help people travel more and create better memories.

So we just kind of fell into blogging. It just felt like a natural fit. I don't think we actually chose it to begin with for its income potential. We wanted it to turn into a profitable business for us and we worked out how to do that along the way. We learned how to create multiple streams of income from blogging. It's a great platform to open up many doors that can bring in income, such as freelance writing, advertising, selling your own products, and speaking.

My teaching experience helped me have the confidence to share my stories and not be afraid to be heard. It also helped me to know how to help others and care about each person's journey, which I think is a huge part of blogging. I had to do a lot of planning, reporting and evaluating with teaching as well, so that's always a skill that helps!

4. How do you evaluate your current situation (financially and emotionally) compared to your "past life"?

OMG! It's a million times better. It has its fair share of challenges, but I wake up every morning totally in control of my day. I do work I love and feel passionately in. I use my experiences to help make a difference in other people's lives. I guess I did that to a certain degree while teaching, but this feels better because I love it more. I feel this is my life's work so I'm fulfilled on so many levels.

I hated teaching and would wake every morning to a screeching alarm and the first word I would say was "Oh f**k." That is no way to live your life.

And financially, I'm making at least double what I would have teaching.

5. If you had to do it all over again, what would you change?

I first had the idea to start a travel blog in 2007. But, I didn't because I believed that no one would want to read what I had to say and Lonely Planet had the market. I still vividly remember the moment where I scrunched up the plans and tossed it in the bin.

Three years of financial hell followed, where I chased ridiculous get rich quick schemes in order to get the money I needed to create a life of travel. In 2010, I finally decided to start the travel blog. And now I have that life of travel.

If I could do it over again, I would have gotten over my doubt and insecurity and started the travel blog at the time when no one really was doing them! Just imagine where we'd be now.

I try not to think too much about that, because regret really serves no purpose. Everything happens for a reason and perhaps starting back then may not have worked anyway because I hadn't yet learned all I needed to know to make it work.

6. Is there anything else you'd like to add based on your experience?

I'd really spend time coming up with a long-term plan and vision. Ensure you have figured out a plan for how you will earn an income and carefully consider where you will travel to and live. We chose possibly the worst country to be a digital nomad in. Australia is super expensive and the internet service is appalling - slow and often no coverage - and very expensive. It's been stressful for us and added a lot of unnecessary pressure. It's so important you research and plan for this before you leave.

SECTION 3

THE TRAVEL PLANNING PHASE

I am a passionate traveler, and from the time I was a child, travel formed me as much as my formal education.
– DAVID ROCKEFELLER

CHAPTER 8
TRAVEL PLANNING

PLANNING YOUR TIME ON THE ROAD

We've already covered a lot of information on how to get you from location dependent to location independent.

Now, where will you go?

How do you decide on that? Maybe you already have enough drive and inspiration to know where you want to go or maybe you are still debating on where would be the best place to travel or base yourself. It's ok either way. The next sections are designed to help you understand how to plan your trip based on what you want and save money along the way.

Need a Bit of Inspiration?

Before moving forward, if you still don't know where you want to go, think again... what do you want? I asked you this at the beginning of this guide because knowing this is essential for all stages of becoming location independent.

But in terms of where to go, if you still don't know, look for some inspiration online. Read travel blogs and see what experiences people are having, look at pictures on Pinterest.com to see how beautiful this world is and discover new places, browse a few magazines, or watch travel-related movies. Inspire yourself and create a connection with these places. This will be the "why" of your desire to go there.

Make your inspiration be the life and purpose of your trip

I believe that the most successful trips are the ones that either have a theme or have a purpose behind them that goes beyond the act of traveling. The reality is that not everyone needs a purpose or theme to travel, but having it will keep you inspired to do more things and keep traveling in the long run. That inspiration will keep your spirit up during the hard times that inevitably come with the travel experience and it will help keep you open to new and foreign experiences.

Some people focus on learning about the culinary approach of different countries, others do yoga, others go volunteering in third world countries, and others challenge themselves to accomplish certain adventures like climbing mountains, exploring natural wonders, and others. Some people also travel to explore themselves, to change the scenery, and to meet new people. No matter what it is, the important thing is that it has to be something that interests you.

During my round the world trip, I've been all about experiencing first hand the architectural wonders I studied in college, living the cultural contrasts and interactions in different parts of the world, and seeing how they affect their current social life. And yes, some adventurous stuff too.

Now, inspiration is not the only thing you need in order to do a proper trip, you need to plan it well in order to have everything (or most of it) under control, have a balance or work and travel, and keep your sanity too! That's what this section will be all about.

To travel is to discover that everyone is wrong about other countries.
– ALDOUS HUXLEY

DECIDING WHERE TO GO

You have the inspiration and by now you should be working on ways of creating your micro-business to make a living on the road.

Ready to start planning your time on the road? This can be either a simple long-term move to a home base on the other side of the world, a semi-nomadic lifestyle, or a fully nomadic trip. It doesn't matter which it is; this planning stage can be quite overwhelming, as you'll need a lot of resources to be able to do it as cheap as possible.

Now the common question is, **where to start?**

It's pretty common to start with one of the two most important aspects of any trip: **destinations** and **budget**. You can start with either one of those, but I like to start with the destinations, as they are deeply related to the inspiration that is driving the trip. The destinations and duration can later be modified when compared to a realistic budget.

So, let's start with destinations for now. I promise we'll get to budgeting soon.

Here are a few important things to take into consideration when deciding where to travel:

Must-Sees and Must-Dos

This is one of the main reasons why you're traveling, right? To see the places you've dreamt about for so long and to do the things you've been piling in your bucket list. The reality is that while you might be able to travel long term, it is just not possible to see *everything* in one trip, so you have to choose wisely.

Do a list of the main things you want to do and places you want to see. You might want to categorize them in **must** and **would love to**. This will help you decide later on which things and places to consider and take out when your plan starts getting in shape.

Also, note in which countries these activities and sights are and map them. You might find that most of them could be in one or two continent, neighboring countries, or in nearby regions. This will help you decide which regions your trip could focus and possibly which route to take.

Cost

As I've demonstrated before, not all destinations cost the same. While you might survive two months in India with $1,500 or less, it is possible that you won't even last two weeks in Australia with the same amount.

You can decide to extend your length of travel by visiting cheaper countries and traveling slow or overland, or you can decide to keep it short. In the end, you have to analyze the cost of each destination you're interested in visiting, the approximate duration in each place, the transportation costs between places, accommodations, among other things, to get an idea of how much a trip like this will cost and how it compares to your budget.

As I recommended before, you can use BudgetYourTrip.com to get a very rough estimate of the cost per day in many countries around the world.

Time

How much time can you spend traveling? Weeks, months, a year, or more? How much time you can dedicate to the trip will somewhat dictate where to go and how many places to visit. Usually, quick trips tend to be more expensive per day since more things and activities are packed into a shorter period. But ideally, you will be able to travel for an indefinite time since you will be sustaining yourself with your micro-business. And speaking of business, how much time of that trip will be spent working? Take that into consideration too.

Travel Method

Along with time, your travel method will dictate how many places to visit and where to go. Do you plan on doing everything overland? In this case, you would possibly be concentrating in a region and keep things cheaper. Do you plan to fly? You could visit more places in a shorter period, but your budget might get consumed with airfares.

It's also important to know that travel options and timeframes vary drastically depending on countries and even continents. For example, train travel in Europe is easy, cost effective, and fast; on the other hand, train travel in Africa might be at a decent price but extremely slow and unreliable. You should take these factors into account when planning.

Logistics

While this is not so common to think about, on certain occasions there is an important logistic in visiting certain countries. For example; when traveling through the Middle East, if you're interested in visiting Lebanon and Israel, you should know that you must visit Lebanon first and then Israel. If you do it the other way, once you're at the Lebanese border the Israeli stamp in your passport will become a problem, and they will not let you enter the country. This also happens with a few other countries due to the Arab League boycott of Israel. Why? It is complex, but let's just say that these countries don't have a good relationship with each other, so they might prevent travelers who visit their "lousy neighbor" from entering their territory.

There are other logistic details to take into consideration, but these should be verified once you have your ideal list of places. For American citizens, it is always good to check the Travel Section of the Department of State website for up to date information on travel requirements, visas, passport, and current alerts. For other nationalities, you can visit your local government immigration or travel site to check this information.

Weather

Do you plan to chase the summer yearlong, or are you looking for some wintertime too? It is always good to know what's the weather like at the time of the year you expect to be at any given destination. This could dictate the type of activities you'll do, what to pack, and even how much to spend, since certain destinations are cheaper during winter or their off-season.

Budget

Lastly, your budget. Estimate how much money you will have to do your trip or to start your location independent life. It could be $10K, $20K, or whatever amount, but you have to be clear on your estimated budget at the time you start your trip and how it is represented in a realistic travel itinerary.

So, let's go deeper into budgeting...

BUDGETING YOUR TRIP

The most important thing when it comes to budgeting is to be realistic and flexible.

While I can't tell you exactly how much your trip will cost, I can help by guiding and telling you what you should consider when budgeting.

You need to be aware that trips cost more than just what you spend on the road. There are pre-trip expenses, trip expenses, and those little hidden expenses that we don't take into account, but that could add up quickly and take us out of budget. Here is a breakdown of the most common expenses:

Pre-trip expenses

These include EVERYTHING you need to get before you start your trip.

- **Passport:** Depending on your country, getting a new

passport or renewing an existing one could cost you around $80 or more. You should also budget for passport pictures (around $5) and other required documents. This has to be done with at least two to three months in advance since this process can take a while, though some countries offer expedited service. Make sure you get all the details about passport applications in your local government's office or website.

- **Visas:** Some countries can require entry visas that can range between $30 and $300. Check with your destination's webpage to see if they require an entry visa.

- **Travel Insurance:** The prices vary depending on the type and extent of insurance you decide to take, the duration, and the place of residence. But to have an idea, basic travel insurance costs between $50 and $80 per month. WorldNomads.com is one of the most trusted travel insurance companies among travelers. Before heading out on the road, get a quote to keep your travels safe.

- **Vaccinations:** Ask your local doctor about the necessary vaccines for the countries you're visiting. Prices vary depending on your place of residence and what you need. A good starting price can be $150+ (especially if you need the Yellow Fever vaccine, which alone can cost more than $100, in the US at least).

- **Backpack:** These can range between $80 and $300+. It all depends on the brand, design, and capacity. A good price range for a decent to good backpack is $100 to $200. I don't recommend spending on an extremely expensive backpack. Expensive doesn't mean it's better. Just get a backpack that fits you and that meets all your needs.

- **Toiletries:** How much you spend on toiletries depends on what you use and like. You can get generic stuff from discount stores like Target and Wal-Mart and save a lot of money, or you can get branded stuff at a higher price. It all depends on you. But a safe range goes between $50 and $100. Keep in mind that you should buy travel size toiletries. First, it won't take much space on your backpack; second, you could take your backpack as a carry-on on your flight.

- **Other Accessories:** Some essentials like a flashlight, poncho, utensils, power converter, money belt, and many other stuff that might be specifically necessary for your trip. A good range can be between $75 and $150.

- **Airplane Ticket:** A good price range for short flights can be between $200 and $600, and long flights between $700 and $1500+. The Airline industry is highly volatile, so prices vary every day. Don't worry; I give you some tips ahead on how to save on airfare.

- **Train Tickets:** This varies depending on your destination and trip duration. Europe has passes that can cost between $300 and $800. United Kingdom has passes for about $200 to $500. United States has passes for $350 to $600. Africa and Asia have really cheap train tickets that can go from $1 to $100+. It all depends on the country and length of the trip.

- **Accommodations:** Good hostels can start from $20 per night and hotels from $60 per night. Of course, the prices vary depending on the city you are visiting, but to have an idea, in my 3+ years of travel all my hostels ranged between $5 to $35 a night.

- **Travel Guides:** Most travel guides range between $15 and $50. LonelyPlanet.com now sells individual chapters. You can buy only the necessary chapters for your destination. Also, not carrying the full guide saves space on your bag.

In general terms, Pre-trip expenses can range between $700 and $2,000+. You can cut some of these expenses by owning already some of the accessories and backpack, and by selecting cheap airfares and accommodation.

Trip Expenses

These are all the expenses you incur while traveling. These are usually budgeted when you plan your trip.

- **Food:** If going to Europe and the United States, a good daily budget is from $25 to $40 depending on what you eat. In some parts of Africa and Asia, it can be from $15 to $25 daily. In Australia and New Zealand, it ranges more around $30 to $45 a day.

- **Local Transportation:** Take into account taxis, subways, trams, buses, regional trains, and other methods of transportation. A good average (depending on the city) can be for about $50 to $150 per week.

- **Going Out:** This budget I leave open to your discretion. If you're a party monster, then budget for beers, nightclub entrance tickets, night cabs, etc. Budget as if you were going out in your city.

- **Sightseeing:** Of course you want to sightsee and go on tours. Since you might not be taking tours every day, I recommend you check online the actual cost of the tours and activities you want to do to budget them properly. You don't need to buy them online, and unless it is necessary, I advise you not to since often they are cheaper when you buy them at the destination. City passes are also good to save money on sightseeing.

- **Souvenirs:** Liked that museum postcard, that necklace, that t-shirt, and many other stuff? Then by all means buy it if you have the money! There is no way to budget accurately for souvenirs since this is something we will not know until we get to the store. But I usually have a budget of $200 (and I'm not a compulsive buyer). This budget depends on your buying trends.

- **Internet:** These days most of us travel with a smart device and use it to stay connected. In many countries, you can buy a pre-paid sim card with 3G for $20 to $40 a month. Otherwise, you can pay for the use of wi-fi or internet connection at internet cafes or other stores and cafes.

Your trip expenses can range between $600 and $1500+. This varies according to destination and length of travel.

Hidden Expenses

These are the expenses we don't usually budget accordingly.

- **WC fee** – Europe is well known for charging between $0.50 and $1.00 for using the restroom. In Asia, it is more like $0.10 to $0.50.

- **Exchange Rate and Fee** – When exchanging money to a different currency, there is an exchange rate that is slightly different than the current exchange rate. This difference is considered the exchange fee. Also, they can charge anything from $0 to $6.00 in commission depending on the amount of money you exchange. It is always recommended to exchange a large amount of money, but only if you expect to use it. Avoid exchanging money at airports and touristic places.

- **ATM Fees** - A good way to "exchange" money is by withdrawing the foreign currency directly from your bank account. Most banks charge close to $5.00 in transaction fees plus a 1% exchange fee (in addition to a fee charged by the ATM bank, which can be around $3 to $5). This option is better than exchanging money if you withdraw a large sum of money from the ATM at once. Some international banks or affiliated banks don't charge the transaction fee if you withdraw on specified banks. Try getting a credit or debit card that charges no foreign transaction fees or that is part of the Global ATM Alliance – which allows you to withdraw money from certain banks without the foreign transaction fee.

- **Train Station Lockers** – Most train stations count with a locker room. Prices can go from $4.00 for small lockers to $8.00 for large lockers. Usually, the rental is for 24 hours.

- **Hostel Towels and Bed Sheets** – Some hostels don't include towels and bed sheets on their prices. These can be up to an extra $5.00 per night.

- **Tips** – The tipping culture varies greatly between countries. People in some countries could feel offended or give you a weird look when you offer a tip while people in other countries will expect a tip and get mad if they don't get it. Check in your travel guide what is the customary tip in your destination. If tipping is customary, then 10% to 15% will do fine.

- **Random Snacks** – We always find some random local snacks we want to try. A budget of $5.00 to $10.00 per day could do more than fine.

- **Laundry** – If you're doing a long duration trip, then you'll do laundry at some point. Budget $10 to $20 per every two weeks for laundry and detergents.

- **Restocking Toiletries** – For long-term travel, add $50 or so per month to restock on your essentials.

- **Medicines**: It happens… you're on the road, and suddenly you get sick and need to buy medicines. We never plan for this, but depending on the situation and place, a visit to the pharmacy could cost a few more dollars than expected.

As you can see, these usually unaccounted expenses can add up to become an essential part of our travel budget. I recommend that after you add ALL of your "expected" pre-trip, trip, and estimated hidden expenses; you should add 5% to 10% of the total amount for any emergency or just to be comfortable and have some wiggle room.

I know that by now it all looks like a huge budget, but ahead in this guide I'll show you how to cut costs and save on several of these items. It is better to budget more first and then fine tune everything to something more manageable, than to under-budget the trip and then feel the pain of not being able to do anything on the road since you didn't save and bring enough money for it.

Did you budget your trip already? Well, pat yourself on the back as your getting closer and closer to that trip. Now, while I told you to budget consciously, have in mind that life on the road is quite dynamic, and sometimes things happen unplanned. There will be times in which you will toss your plans and go on a different path, and that's totally ok. Just have in mind that once you do that, you should re-budget to be conscious about how much you'll spend and how can you manage it with your current income.

―――――――――

Wherever you go, go with all your heart.
― CONFUCIUS

―――――――――

SELECTING THE BEST TRAVEL INSURANCE

In general, travel insurance is intended to cover the financial default or negligence of travel suppliers, unexpected medical expenses, and other losses incurred while traveling. These situations can happen either on a domestic trip (traveling in one's own country) or internationally.

Something I want to stress is that travel insurance is NOT a replacement to your regular health insurance as it is designed to cover you for **unexpected** emergencies that might occur in the course of your trip.

To prove the point, in 2011 I failed to get travel insurance when I went to Honduras (I didn't want to pay it and was too lazy to research it). When I was in the Mayan ruins of Copan Ruinas I fell from the pyramid and cut open my knee. I was afraid of going to the hospital fearing they could charge me a lot for the visit. Luckily I was able to manage without going to the hospital thanks to a very nice lady I met there and offered to help.

As you might know, the travel insurance industry is a giant and profitable monster with multiple entities offering multiple coverage options. Without a doubt, it can be extremely confusing to select the right plan for you. But here are some things you should consider when comparing policies.

Does it cover you?

The first thing you need to have in mind is that many travel insurance companies only provide insurance regionally;

meaning, only to citizens of the US and Canada, or Australians, or in the UK. Once you know it covers you based on your citizenship and residence, you can go on to study the coverage details.

Extent of Coverage

Read even the small prints to **know exactly what is covered, what's not, and how much will it cover?** Is it only medical insurance or does it also covers your trip expenses in case of cancellations and theft of personal items like electronics? Will it cover if you accidentally break your camera?

I once bought a policy and failed to notice that it was only medical. When I got my iPod stolen at the Pyramids of Giza, I went through the annoying process of getting a "dubious" police report, only to be told afterwards by my insurance company that it wasn't covered. Wah, wah... (Now that I think about it, there's something about pyramids that gets me in trouble!)

If it covers your personal possessions, under what circumstances are they covered? Will it cover your backpack if it gets stolen on the street while unattended, or if taken from a hostel locker, or lost in transit? While the end result is the same –losing your backpack– not all scenarios are equal to the insurance company, and not all of them might be covered.

Most travel insurance policies won't cover theft caused by your negligence or by leaving things "unattended".

As said before, coverage varies depending on the policy, but these are the most common risks that are covered by most travel insurance policies:

- **Delayed departure and missed connection due to airlines schedule** – Gives compensation for any money lost due to a delayed departure that overpasses a given amount of time.

- **Trip cancellation and interruption** – If due to unforeseen circumstances you have to cancel your trip early, you will be compensated for any monies lost.

- **Travel delays due to weather** – Many insurance policies can cover weather up to a certain degree.

- **Delayed, lost, stolen, or damaged baggage, personal effects, or travel documents** – Protects your possessions and gives you the possibility to claim any compensation for stolen or lost items. In many cases, it also covers any administrative costs incurred in the event that your passport is stolen and needs to be reissued. Some insurance policies will also compensate you for any stolen cash or travelers' cheques, up to a certain limit.

- **Legal assistance and personal liability** – This is a legal cover for any accident, injury, or harm you might inadvertently inflict on another individual.

- **Medical and dental expenses** – Covers the money you spent on medical and dental expenses. Note that this is not for regular checkups, only for *unexpected* urgent care or emergencies.

- **Medical emergency and hospital care (Accident or Sickness)** – This will provide financial cover for any payments you have to make in the event that you need medical attention.

- **Emergency evacuation, rescue, and repatriation of remains** – Your insurer will pay all your costs in the event of a medical emergency rescue or the repatriation of remains.

- **Accidental death, injury, or disablement benefit** – Covers you or a beneficiary in case of physical injury and death. In many cases, it also covers overseas funeral expenses.

Medical Coverage and Evacuation

It is really important to take a close look at the medical insurance policy, as this is the main or most important reason you're getting travel insurance.

Does it cover pre-existing conditions? Most travel insurances don't cover them. For example, if you know you have asthma, and you suffer from an attack, you're not going to be covered.

Do they offer a separate "pre-existing conditions" coverage? If they do, which ones are covered?

What are the maximum hospital emergencies coverage limits? Hospital costs for emergencies are extremely expensive in most countries. Know the maximum coverage limits and know who disburses the money to the hospital during the emergency; you (to be later reimbursed by the travel insurance), or if the insurance covers it initially.

The "Emergency Medical" coverage limit is related to the amount of money you pay for the coverage. A limit of $50,000 will surely pay less than a limit of $1,000,000.

When you are selecting your policy, you can see the price you'll pay depending on the "Emergency Medical" coverage you choose to have.

My personal recommendation is to have a limit of at least $100,000. You don't want to run out of "insurance money" half way of your emergency procedure or recovery.

How much will your copayment be? As with the "Emergency Medical "limit, the amount of copayment can vary according to the price you pay .Copayments can go from $0 (most expensive policy) to $500 and more .I usually prefer to pay more (about $20 more for a three months policy) to have a $0 copayment vs. a $250 copayment.

Is it primary or secondary coverage? The difference between primary and secondary is who pays the hospital or doctor .With primary travel insurance, you will be provided an insurance card you can present at the hospital .If accepted, the insurance will pay directly the hospital, and you'll only have to pay the copayment (if any .(With the secondary, on the other hand, you'll have to pay ALL expenses and the insurance will refund you back the money if it is covered (except excess and copayment.(

Will they cover emergency medical evacuation? Your insurer will pay all your costs in the event of a medical emergency rescue, which by itself can cost $10,000 and more for the helicopter (if you're in a remote location) or other transportation.

Additional Coverage

There are chances the policy you're interested in will not include everything you want to cover. In these cases, **do they have "additional coverage" add-on's and for how much?**

Typical add-on's are:

- **Car rental collision coverage**
- **Pre-existing conditions** – discussed above.
- **Sports considered having a high risk** – for example, scuba diving, skiing, and others. (More on this below)
- **Travel to high-risk countries** – Certain countries might not be included due to volatile politics, war, natural disasters, or acts of terrorism.
- **Additional accidental death and dismemberment coverage** – upgrade the limit to this coverage.
- **Kidnap and ransom insurance**
- **3rd party supplier insolvency** – In cases when the hotel or airline to which you made non-refundable payments has gone into bankruptcy or liquidation and ceased to offer their services.

Cancellation

Make sure that your policy has cancellation insurance. If it does, what types of cancellations does it cover? **Does it cover if you have to suddenly cancel due to work? Or if a family member dies or gets sick? Or if you get sick?** If it does cover, what and how much does it cover?

An important note on this specific coverage. For it to apply, it *must* be acquired at the same time you purchase (or given timeframe) your plane tickets, tour, or other. You cannot purchase it right before canceling.

Price

Price is obviously high on the list of consideration on every budget traveler and with all honesty, the price is one of the main factors I have in mind when I choose my policy. Still, when comparing travel insurance, don't focus only on the lowest price. Compare the price alongside with what's covered. You might notice that a specific insurance might be slightly more expensive than the other, but the coverage might be substantially better. Look at it as a return on investment (ROI). For example, I pay $20 more, but I get $50,000 more in emergency medical coverage.

As a rule of thumb, the insurance policy price should not be more than 7% of the total cost of your trip.

Activities Covered

Not all policies are designed the same way. What sort of traveler are you? Do you like extreme sports? Are you visiting "dangerous" countries? Are you doing a remote expedition?

Not all policies cover injuries incurred from extreme sports and even certain regular sports. As an example, WorldNomads.com will not cover you if you get injured while Base Jumping, but it does cover you in case of an injury while Bungee Jumping or other sports.

If you know the activities you'll be doing while on your trip (especially extreme sports), research if your policy covers them.

How to Make Claims

Know the procedure necessary to make a claim. **Is it easy? How long does it take? How can they be contacted?** Are they available 24/7? Can the claim be submitted online? What proof is needed and other documentation to make the claim?

You can know all this by contacting the underwriter of your policy with all these questions. They will let you know the right procedure to make claims.

Countries Covered

Today, most travel insurance provide coverage for most countries in the world. But, there are a few countries that are not covered for different reasons, whether it's due to political unrest, current danger towards foreign visitors, or for other reasons. Always make sure you verify the list of countries covered by the policy against the list of countries your visiting. It will suck if you spend your money on an insurance that is worthless in the country you're visiting.

Liability

Accidents do happen, and when they do, it's always good to know who's liable.

You are in a ceramics store and knock over an expensive figurine with your backpack. The figurine fell on someone's foot, injuring him or her. Will you have to pay for the medical expenses of that person out of your pocket (and pay for the figurine too)? Well, probably yes. But, **will your travel insurance refund you?** Read very closely if the policy includes personal liability coverage and who is liable under different types of accidents.

What's Not Covered

While all travel insurances will tell you what they include, many of them *will not* tell you what they *don't* include. In general, these are conditions that most travel insurances will not cover you:

- **Deliberately putting your life in danger** – Activities that put your life in extreme danger or that injury is likely are often not covered.

- **HIV or other STD's** – Whether acquired through protected or unprotected sex or other methods. Travel Insurances cover no STDs.

- **Injury or illness caused by alcohol or drug use** – This is a claim often submitted by travelers and declined by the insurance. When under the influences of drugs or alcohol, you are prone to take more risks since you are not in your "full capabilities to be in control".

- **Illegal Activities** – Illegal activities vary from country to country, so if you are involved in illegal activity, even if unknowingly, your travel insurance will not cover you in case of an emergency.

- **War or terrorism** – While most plans might not cover this, some do cover this risk as an additional coverage.

How to Buy?

Now that you know what to look, how do you look for it and select the best policy? This is the process I take when I choose to buy my travel insurance.

- I identify the type of coverage I need for my trip based on all the points mentioned above. For example: I need emergency medical of at least $100,000; Evacuation; I need it to cover me in Italy, Morocco, Tunisia; I want to pay $0 copayment and I want it to be primary coverage. (among other details)

- I calculate the total overall trip expenses if I want the insurance to cover for any unexpected cancellation. During my round the world I've chosen to skip this step since I'm doing things on the go, so I don't have a big amount of money on risk of cancellation.

- I research for the best travel insurance. Popular among backpackers is WorldNomads.com. I like them because they are really good, easy to submit claims, have a very extensive coverage for residents of over 150 countries, and their list of covered countries (to travel to) is also very extensive. That being said, they are not the cheapest, but they are still affordable. For other policies, I tend to use SquareMouth.com, where you just put some basic information, and it will show you dozens of policies that apply to you. I've found this site super convenient to compare side-by-side different policies. The buying process is extremely quick and smooth too.

And voila… I'm insured!

When not to buy travel insurance?

Ok, not that I'm saying you should travel uninsured, but it is possible you could already be fully or partially insured and not know about it. Some credit cards, like American Express, or certain health insurance providers could offer some coverage while abroad. Just read the small print or contact them to see what and how much is covered, if they do. Should you have some coverage, all you need to do is complement what you're lacking with additional travel insurance.

Finally, I want to stress **the importance of reading the small prints!** It is a common mistake (as I mentioned above from experience) to purchase travel insurance without reading the details, only to find out later that you are not covered for that situation.

VACCINES

Most people don't think of this, but vaccinating is an important aspect of travel planning, especially if you're visiting countries that have a "disease alert."

The Center for Disease and Prevention has an excellent travel section that gives current information on any required and recommended vaccines according to the countries you're visiting, and any travel health notices that you might need to consider or be aware of in order to be prepared. You can visit CDC.gov, select the countries you're visiting, and read all the information pertinent to those countries. Make a list of all the vaccines you need and visit your primary doctor or nearest travel doctor to get the new vaccines and renew the old ones (as necessary).

Some countries that have a "Yellow Fever Alert" do require a Yellow Fever vaccination proof to let you in (often a yellow card with the vaccination record). In some cases, if you've traveled previously to a country where there's Yellow Fever or even the risk of Yellow Fever, you will be asked to show proof that you're vaccinated once you arrive at the next destination; otherwise they will deny your entry. The Yellow Fever vaccination lasts ten years. You can go to CDC.gov to know the regions with risk of Yellow Fever.

Some shots you should consider having up to date are Yellow Fever, Hepatitis A, Hepatitis B, Meningitis, Polio, Tetanus booster, Typhoid/Diphtheria, and MMR booster.

Consider carrying Malaria pills if you're traveling to a country in a "Malaria zone". While they are not 100% effective, they will reduce your chances of contracting Malaria. You can check CDC.gov to see the Malaria Zones across the world.

Another great page to look at for current health information is the World Health Organization's Country-specific Reports. (http://www.who.int/countries/en/)

UNDERSTANDING PASSPORTS AND VISAS

If you're planning an international trip, you must be aware that you will need to have a passport, and depending on your destination, you might need a visa too. I'll explain how both of these documents work to help you understand how to use and get both of them, and when are they necessary.

I want to note that while this information will be mostly focused towards US citizens, I will mention other international samples that might be relevant.

Passports

I want to start with a fun fact. Did you know that passports are much older than you might think? One of the earliest samples of a "passport" is mentioned in the Hebrew Bible, stating that Nehemiah (about 450 BC in Persia) had the king's permission to travel to Judea with safe passage. Later, in the medieval Islamic Caliphate, a form of passport was the *bara'a*, which was actually a receipt for taxes paid. Only citizens who paid their taxes were permitted to travel to different regions of the Caliphate.

The word passport comes from a medieval document that was required to pass through the gate ("porte") of the city wall or to pass through a territory.

These days, though, a passport is required for all international travel. If you're a US Citizen, you can travel all around the United States and its territories without a passport, but once you decide to cross international lines (like going to Mexico), a passport will be required.

Certain international countries create "free trade/movement regions," which allows citizens of the countries in each region to cross borders with just an ID. Among these regions are *Mercosur* in South America, *Schengen* in Europe, and the *East African Community* in Africa, including many others.

Passports are the only universally accepted identification, so having a passport is crucial for international travel. Equally, a passport is crucial to be able to depart the international destination and re-enter your country of origin. It is a form of keeping an accurate track of where you've been.

Since July 2008, the U.S. State Department began producing two types of Passports: Passport Book and Passport Card. Passport Cards are not valid for international air travel but may be used for land and sea travel between the US, Canada, Mexico, Bermuda and The Caribbean. The Passport Book is valid for any international travel.

How To Apply For A US Passport (US Citizens)

If you are applying for your first US Passport, then you must apply in person at any regional passport agency or other facilities that accepts passports applications (like certain post offices and courthouses). You can find the nearest agency or facility with the U.S. State Department website's search tool on travel.state.gov.

You will need to fill out the DS-11 form (available online), provide proof of US citizenship, proof of identity with a driver's license or government ID, two 2x2 passport photos, and your social security number. Note: Don't sign the form until you are in the presence of an authorized executing official.

You can apply or renew by mail if you've had a passport in the past 15 years and had 16 years or more when the passport was issued. When renewing by mail, you will need to mail also your previous passport.

For renewals, fill out the DS-82 form, which is available on the U.S. Department of State website. Sign and date it.

Make sure you start the process at least 2 to 3 months in advance of your planned trip, as the average processing time takes six weeks. If you need your passport as soon as possible, you can have it expedited for an additional $60 and can receive it within two weeks. Make sure you label the application with EXPEDITED. If you need it even sooner than that, you can pay for overnight delivery.

The current costs new passports and renewals can be found on the US Department of State website.

For other countries, you should visit your government's immigration website or local office. Should you not know the URL for the website, you can Google "new passport application in [name of country]," which will probably show you the correct page. Check there the application procedure, requirements, and costs.

Visas

Different to passports, visas vary drastically depending on the type of passport you carry and the country you're visiting. A visa is a document indicating that a person is authorized to enter the country for a specific period of time. These documents are often in the form of stamps or stickers placed in your passport. For example, someone traveling to Russia with a US passport will need to get a visa, but someone traveling to Russia with a Brazilian passport will not need it.

There are more than a dozen types of visas, but they can be generally classified as immigrant visas and non-immigrant visas. Non-immigrant visas are usually for tourist and business visitors.

When required, the country issuing the visa typically attaches various conditions to the visa, such as the time when the visa is valid, the period of time that the person may stay in the country, whether the visa is valid for more than one visit, and more. For example, my Brazilian Visa (with a US passport) is valid for 10 years, allowing me to stay for up to 180 days per year, with multiple entries to the country within those 10 years.

Regarding business visas in relation to being location independent or digital nomad. In theory, any person doing business in any country will need to apply for a business visa to conduct their business there. While this is true, to this day I've worked pretty much in most countries I've visited and have applied for a total of zero business visas. (And I'm sure 95% of travel bloggers and digital nomads stand in the same boat.)

It's not that I'm illegal, but being a digital nomad has its gray areas that are beneficial. In my case, I'm working with my computer in any given country, but I'm not doing business with a local or selling anything locally. For that reason, I'm not doing business in/with that country.

While the law in each country is different, many countries fall under the umbrella of "you're still a tourist as long as you don't do your business with a local or sell locally." That being said, I'm not a legal expert, so check the law before you go (but honestly, there's not much to fuss about if you're making a living *solely* online). So, when applying for a visa, depending on your business circumstances, you can simply say you're there for tourism and keep your business to yourself.

Understand your visa requirements

A visa will influence your trip's timeline and dictate for how long you can stay in a country according to your passport's nationality. Not all passports are created equally, and some offer more freedom than others. If you want to know specific details about your passport, including a list of countries that require visas, among other information; search for it on Wikipedia or your local government's travel/immigration page.

- US citizens, go to the Department of State's Travel Page for visa requirement information. http://travel.state.gov/
- Canadian citizens can find it in the travel section of Government of Canada site. http://travel.gc.ca/
- UK citizens should visit the travel section of Gov.uk for travel and visa information. https://www.gov.uk/browse/abroad

- Australians should visit the Department of Foreign Affairs and Trade's site. http://www.dfat.gov.au/visas/

- New Zealand citizens can see their visa requirements via the dedicated Wikipedia page.

- For all other citizens, including the above, IATATravelCentre.com has a great database and so does Visahq.com (which also offer a service to apply for the visa). Equally, you can search on Wikipedia for "visa requirements for [country] citizens."

How To Apply For A Visa

Many countries like Tunisia, Peru, Thailand, most European countries, and many others, will let you enter "visa free" with just a valid passport and the return flight information, and they usually let you stay between 30 to 90 days (with a US passport or a passport from most first world countries. Other passport holders may need to get a visa to enter these countries).

Some countries, such as Egypt and Kenya, will allow you to enter with a "visa on arrival" that you pay once you arrive at the airport or when you cross the land border.

Other countries, like Russia and Kazakhstan, will require you to obtain a visa before departing your country of residence or previous destination. In these cases, you need to head to your nearest embassy or consulate of the destination country and apply there.

Visa requirements change constantly, but to know the current requirements, check the US Department of State Travel Page for all the entry and exit requirements. Other passport holders can check their own government's immigration or travel page for these details.

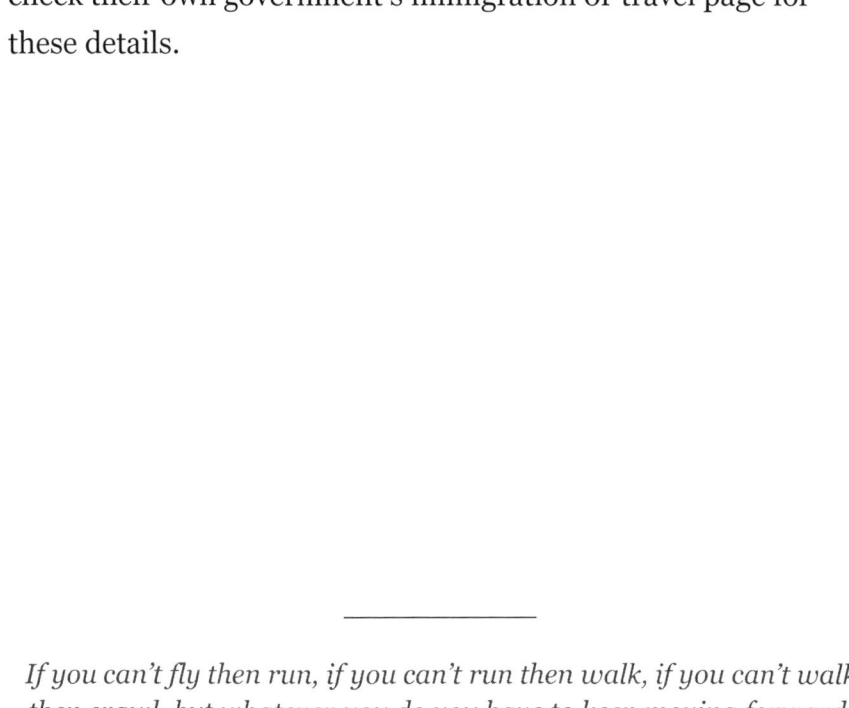

If you can't fly then run, if you can't run then walk, if you can't walk then crawl, but whatever you do you have to keep moving forward.
– MARTIN LUTHER KING JR.

ROUND THE WORLD AIRFARES OR POINT BY POINT TICKETS?

Round the world travelers get faced with this question all the time. Should I buy point-by-point airfares or a Round the World (RTW) ticket? I have gone with the point-by-point method because I love the freedom and flexibility of staying longer in certain places or changing my route as many times as I want according to the experiences I'm having or any other form of inspiration I get on the road.

Still, I am aware RTW tickets are really good to save money on airfare if you have a structured itinerary and plan on following it. RTW tickets do still allow for some flexibility changing your departure dates as long as it follows their terms, keeps the same route, and falls within the 12 months validity of the ticket. The beauty of RTW tickets is that you might probably be able to visit more places with cheaper airfare since you're locking all your airfare prices way in advance.

Having said that, if you're an excellent travel hacker (we'll get into that soon), you know that sometimes you can find dirt-cheap flights that can beat the price of any RTW ticket.

RTW tickets work based on airline alliances. A group or airlines come together and share (in many cases) their routes, ticket platform, and more. Once you select an alliance, you can see all the places you can visit within their network. Have in mind that different alliances visit different countries, so if you'd like to visit a country that is not covered by your alliance of choice, you can either consider another alliance or buy that leg of the trip as a separate ticket and return to your alliance RTW ticket after it.

The three main RTW alliances are:

- *StarAlliance.com*
- *OneWorld.com*
- *SkyTeam.com*

The following companies, while not alliances themselves, can help you create a RTW itinerary or simply book separate itineraries. The good thing about them is that they don't restrict your flight per alliance, so you have more wiggle room to play.

- *Airtreks.com* – the leader in RTW planning
- *BootnAll.com* – Also a good alternative.

Travel is fatal to prejudice, bigotry, and narrow-mindedness, and many of our people need it sorely on these accounts. Broad, wholesome, charitable views of men and things cannot be acquired by vegetating in one little corner of the earth all one's lifetime.
– MARK TWAIN

FINDING LONG TERM ACCOMMODATION

Finding a cheap hotel or hostel is not that hard. My recommendation is to search on the list of sites below and pick on your preferred accommodation depending on price, location, and quality.

Hotels:

- *Booking.com* (often offers really cheap accommodation options)
- *Hotels.com*
- *Expedia.com*
- *Agoda.com* (highly recommended)
- *Priceline.com* (where you can bid for lower prices)
- *Hotwire.com* (get lower prices but don't know the hotel name until after you pay)

Hostels:

- *HostelWorld.com* (biggest hostel selection)
- *HostelBookers.com* (sometimes cheaper)
- *Hostels.com*

BUT, when it comes to long-term accommodation, these hotels and hostels might not be the best choices. You want to be more comfortable, right? When it comes to long-term accommodation, my preferred choice is airbnb.com. They have over a million location options that range from rooms to apartments, full houses, and even boats, which you can rent for a few days or even a few months.

I've used AirBnb in several countries and I've loved every single experience and location. The site has a review system where you can see how the previous guests liked or disliked the place. And more often than not, the price is much lower than a hotel or hostel, but with more comforts of a real place to live (like a kitchen!).

I've also found long-term apartment rentals by searching around locally after I arrive at the city, either by asking around or by searching in local newspapers or searching online for apartment rentals in that city.

Another option, which I haven't tried to date but I'm still curious to try it, is house sitting. This option allows you to stay at someone's place for free in exchange for taking care of it or their pets while the owners are away. I can't say much about this option since I haven't tried it personally, but I'm going to recommend you to check GlobetrotterGirls.com to learn more about it since they have mastered this art of free accommodation.

One final tip... if you don't know where in the city to get a long term apartment/accommodation, try CouchSurfing.org for the first few days in the city. This will allow you to get to know it a bit through your own experience and your host's recommendations. Then, you can search for your own place with better knowledge of the city and what's around each neighborhood.

ESTABLISHING YOUR BANKING FOR THE ROAD

Banking on the road is not that much different than banking at home; you can still use your debit and credit cards for most purchases out there unless you're in an undeveloped country that is mostly a cash economy.

Notify Your Bank

Before you start your trip, you should notify your bank about your travel plans. Call and let them know when and where will you be traveling so they don't block your account/credit card thinking your purchase abroad is suspicious activity. Also, confirm with your bank about the possibility of having a new credit/debit card shipped to you at your new destination should you lose it on the road.

Not all banks do this, so in case they don't, you can ask for a duplicate card before you leave home. This you can keep hidden somewhere safe and use only in case you lose your primary card.

Get a Travel-Friendly Debit Card

When you withdraw money abroad, you will get charged an ATM fee as well as your bank's fee for withdrawing outside their network.

For US and international based travelers, I recommend checking the Global ATM Alliance to see if your bank doesn't charge to withdraw from any of the banks on the list (or to open an account with any of them if your bank is not on the list). And to US based travelers I recommend opening a Schwab Bank Checking Account linked to a Schwab One brokerage account, which allow you to withdraw money from any bank without any outside network fee, and they refund you the fee charged by the foreign bank. This is the debit card I use everywhere.

Certain banks, like CitiBank and HSBC, have international branches all around the world; so for example, if you have CitiBank debit card, you wouldn't pay a fee to withdraw money from any CitiBank ATM around the world.

Should you not be able to get a travel-friendly debit card, only withdraw money abroad when necessary and the largest amount allowable by your bank or the ATM. Why? Your bank will charge you a fixed amount of dollars for the transaction plus a percentage of the amount withdrawn, in addition to the fixed amount charged by the ATM's bank. Usually, these can add up to $10+ per withdrawal. So, you minimize that loss by withdrawing the largest amount possible, so you need to do fewer withdrawals during your trip.

Always Hunt for the Best Exchange Rate

Should you have a "no fee" debit card, you should try to always withdraw money from an ATM with your debit card since that will be the most accurate and best exchange rate you'll get anywhere.

Should you have cash that you'd like to exchange, try to carry only the most "liquid" currencies in the market, which are the US

Dollar, the British Pound, and the Euro. If you exchange from these currencies to the local currency, you'll get a better exchange rate since they have a good "flow" and demand. Other currency pairs (like Egyptian Pound to Thai Bahts) will charge a ridiculously high commission since that pair exchange has a low demand.

Never exchange money at the airport since they are the gateway to the country, so they know people will need money to pay for a taxi, public transportation, or such. Only withdraw from an ATM. If you have to exchange money at the airport, only exchange the minimum amount possible to get you to the city, and there you will look at different exchange kiosks to compare their buy/sell exchange rates. I use the XE.com app to keep track of the current exchange rate of any currency, so if I have to exchange money, I can compare the kiosk's rate to the real rate and see how much money I'm losing just because I need to exchange. Of course, the closest the exchange rate you see on the kiosk is to the rate on the app, the better it is for you.

Don't Carry Travelers Cheques

Before the 2000s, travelers cheques were a popular form of payment, and they were accepted everywhere. Today, you don't see them anymore, and most places don't even accept them, so don't bother carrying them.

Get a Credit Card with Zero International Transaction Fees

When making purchases in a foreign country, many credit cards charge a small percentage of the purchase to make the international transaction possible. This is unnecessary since you can easily get a credit card that charges 0% on international transactions, so you will be paying only the cost of the item purchased (converted into your currency).

For a few years, I used the Capital One Venture card because it offered zero international transaction fees. But now, I'm using the Chase Sapphire Preferred because, in addition to the zero international transaction fees, it offers an excellent rewards program for travel hacking.

HOW TO FIND A GOOD TRAVEL CREDIT CARD

A good travel credit card is not just any credit card. These are credit cards designed specifically to minimize our foreign transaction fees and maximize our travel and purchase rewards.

You should use a travel credit card for any purchase possible, big or small, to rack up on those bonus miles and points the issuer gives per dollar spent. But, you should *only* use it if you have the money to pay the credit card in full. Otherwise, it won't make sense to earn miles when you're paying interest on the purchases. It is simply not sustainable.

What should you look for in a travel credit card?

Since there is no single answer when selecting credit cards, you should sit, search, and brainstorm what are the benefits you would like to have as a traveler. After that, categorize them from most important to least. Here are some features you could look for when searching for that travel credit card:

Type of Credit Card – Today, the world is mostly dominated by three major credit cards companies: Visa, Master Card, American Express. Choosing between those three will almost guarantee you of having a reliable credit card anywhere in the world. I recommend that when traveling; take at least two credit cards from two different issuers. In case they don't accept one issuer at one retail location, you have the other one for backup.

Affiliation – Some cards affiliated with hotels can offer you discounts, upgrades, or even a free night stay when you use the card at their location. The same goes for other companies like car rentals, stores, airlines, etc.

Sign-up Bonus – Many credit cards have HUGE sign-up bonus, especially if they are affiliated with an airline. Many of them offer up to 50,000 points/miles after your first purchase (that alone is enough for a free round-trip ticket from the US to Europe). Check out for credit cards affiliated with the airlines of your choice. Obviously, an airline you know you could constantly use or that is based close to where you live. If none of those apply to you, then you should consider American Airlines (One World), United Airlines (Star Alliance), and Delta Airlines (SkyTeam).

This also applies to hotels.

Rewards Program – Rewards are really important when selecting a credit card. A good reward program can save you hundreds of dollars in future travels or everyday purchases. Many credit cards give you 1 point (or "x" amount) for everyday purchases, and double or triple points for travel purchases, gas, groceries, and some limited items.

Rewards Usability – Some cards have certain limits on when and where you can travel with your rewards points. Avoid cards that tie you up to specific merchants (like, you can only use your points with one company) or that have many blackout dates.

Annual Fee – Even when we don't like annual fees, often the best rewards programs and best benefits are found in credit cards with annual fees. Compare if paying those $25-$90 dollars a year is worth it for you based on the estimated amount of points you believe you'll earn. Just a recommendation... If you travel a lot, it is worth it.

Often, cards with annual fee offer their first year without the fee. In these cases, you could apply for the card, use it for the first year to earn the bonus miles and any other purchase miles, and then before the year ends (the date in which you opened the account) you can cancel the card with no problem. If you were accumulating airline miles, you wouldn't lose your miles since they are accumulated in your frequent flyer program, instead of your credit card account. But, if you're accumulating point to be used through your credit card, then you should be aware that you'll lose those points.

Conversion Rate – Previously I wrote about reward points. One thing is to earn a lot of reward points, and another thing is the price point of reward redemption. You can earn 2 points per dollar on your purchases (which can add to a lot, and quick) but if the conversion rate is really high (meaning, you need to get 100,000 points to convert your point into flights, hotel stays, etc.) then it might not be that good of a deal for you. On the other hand, you might have another card that gives similar points per dollar and the redemption point for your desired flight is 30,000 points. This will be much more desirable since you have a better return on investment.

Fees – Yes, all those hidden fees and interest charges... ALWAYS read the fine prints. Fees for international purchases can range between 2% to 5%+ of the purchase price. Some even charge additional fees. The best travel credit cards have *zero* international transaction fees.

Insurance – Many credit cards offer some sort of travel insurance and/or "purchase" insurance. Ask the credit card company what benefits they offer. This is one of the reasons why I use my credit card for many of my travel purchases. The complementary insurance on car rentals and trip cancellation or delays can be a lifesaver. Also, most credit cards these days help resolve fraudulent charges, should they happen when abroad.

While I would like to recommend directly a specific credit card, based on the ones I use, the truth is that the sign-up bonuses and offers change all the time. But as I mentioned before, I currently use as my primary card the Chase Sapphire Premier Card.

ADDITIONAL SMALL DETAILS TO COVER BEFORE DEPARTING

Scan and PDF your important documents: This includes passports, IDs, driver's license, and other documents. Send them to yourself by email or place them in Dropbox.com or other cloud services. It's good to have digital copies of them in case they get lost on the road.

Get a Google Voice number (mostly for US-based travelers) and a Skype account: Google Voice gives you a free phone number to receive and make free calls from/to the US. International calls are very cheap too. You can also receive emails of voicemail transcripts or texts messages.

Skype.com is a similar tool available internationally and it doesn't depend on a phone number, though should you need it, you can pay about $6 per month to have a Skype phone number where people can call you too. They are excellent tools for when you need to call your bank from abroad, your parents, or simply to stay in touch.

Back up your laptop or mobile device: If you are traveling with your laptop or mobile device, consider backing up your photos and files online. It's good to have an external hard drive to backup, but if something happens on the road, and your backpack gets stolen, at least your pictures and files will be safe online.

These companies backup your laptop to the cloud:

- *Carbonite.com*
- *Crashplan (code42.com)*
- *Mozy.com*

Change your snail-mail to a new address: You're going to be on the road for a long time, yet you'll still receive letters from your bank, magazine subscriptions, and any other form of snail mail. Before leaving, you should convert as much as possible all this mail into paperless, so it is delivered directly to your email, and cancel any subscriptions that are not necessary. But if these are not an option, you can change your mailing address to your parents' home (or any other close relative or friend you trust). They can receive the mail and read to you or scan any essential letters.

Otherwise, there are services like:

- US Addresses: *EarthClassMail.com*
- EU Addresses: *SwissPostBox.com*
- UK Addresses: *UKPostBox.com*
- AU Addresses: *AusPost.com.au*

Should you not want to use any of the options mentioned above, you can ask for your mail to be stored at your local post office for a defined amount of time. Then, it will all be delivered one day after you return home. This service has a fee that varies per country, so you should visit your local postal service website to get the current rates.

IN THEIR OWN WORDS

DAVE BOUSKILL & DEBRA CORBEIL

Originally from: Canada

Website: ThePlanetD.com

1. What did you do before traveling (particularly to make a living) and what made you decide to become location independent?

Before our travel careers, we both worked in the film business in Toronto, Canada. There were many feature films shooting here and Dave worked as the head of the lighting department in feature films such as The Incredible Hulk, Silent Hill and Chicago. I worked as a makeup artist on Canadian TV series and networks. Most movies film in Toronto from Spring to Autumn, so our winters were usually down time. Instead of staying in the city, we left to travel. Every time we left, we came back yearning to stay on the road. We did trips from 5 weeks to 7 months over the course of 8 years before finally taking the plunge.

2. How did you deal with different aspects of becoming location independent? (emotionally, socially, and financially)

Luckily we had each other so emotionally we had a great support system. You go through a lot of emotions when you first start traveling. Once the honeymoon is over, reality sets in and you have to start to think about money and the future. We had a plan before leaving for good in 2009. We spent 2008 living frugally and working hard. Luckily you can put away a lot of cash in the movie business quickly if you don't have a lot of expenses. My parents were nice enough to let us stay in their trailer that they used to take to Florida, so we didn't have to worry about rent. We put away around $20,000 to last us on the road. We never did touch our investments or savings, so that gave us a nice cushion to pursue our careers until an income started to come in. $20,000 doesn't last forever on the road though, so we really needed to start making money after a few months. When we sold our first set of ads in Sri Lanka, we started to feel a lot better.

Our friends and family were so used to us traveling over the years, our social lives didn't change much. The film business is all consuming so when you are working on a movie, you don't have much of a social life. Once the movie was finished, we'd take off for a few weeks or months, so for nearly 8 years of our lives, friends and family were used to not seeing us a lot. The Internet and social media evolved a lot during that time so we found that we were calling home and chatting with friends and family more than ever!

3. What prompted you to choose this specific path of income and how did your previous job help you get there?

It was our passion for travel that prompted our move. I remember sitting on a bus in Laos in 2003 and dreading having to come home to go back to a job that I wasn't passionate about. I said to Dave "I wish we could do this forever and have a purpose to our travels." We started looking for ways to make travel a career from that moment on. We started working on our dive masters because we thought that would be a great way to work and travel. We looked into running cycling tours and we even considered buying a beach bar. It was our background in the film business that really got the creative juices going through.

After 4 years of looking into different things, we decided that we should pitch a travel show about a regular every day couple doing extraordinary adventures together. We signed up for the Tour d'Afrique: the world's longest cycling race from Cairo to Cape Town. We decided that we needed to do something epic to stand apart from other travellers and this would make for a great pilot to our TV show. We hired a publicist and gained a lot of media exposure. But we weren't a well-known enough brand so when we returned from Africa, it didn't take off. We then decided that we had to build our brand and profile so we looked into creating an online C.V. to house our videos, photos and writing all in one place. And that's when we discovered blogging. We found that we loved travel blogging and being in charge of our own destiny so we focused on building that. And the rest is history.

4. How do you evaluate your current situation (financially and emotionally) compared to your "past life"?

We are leaps and bounds ahead emotionally. We have time together, we have fun together and we have a passion for what we do. Funny enough, we are now better off financially too. We've been doing this for 6 years and it is true what they say. "When you love what you do, the money will come." Instead of going into this career for the money (unlike our previous professions), we went into it because we loved it and we were passionate about travel, adventure, and being together. We now make more money through our travel blog than we did in the film business. It's funny because we went into the film business for the big money, and went into travel blogging not for the money at all, but for the quality of life. We had a mission to show people that you can live an extraordinary life and we wanted to inspire others to follow their dreams. By doing this job for all the right reasons, the financial gain eventually came.

5. If you had to do it all over again, what would you change?

I wouldn't change much. It has been a wild and fun ride. We've made a lot of mistakes, but we've learned from them and moved on. I think mistakes are important. They make you push forward and create different ways to make things work. Everyone has their own path, if you follow your heart, you'll get there eventually. It took us a bit longer than other people, but once success happened (both in life and career) we were ready to embrace it. If we didn't make mistakes, we would take it for granted. We don't take one moment for granted. We know we are lucky to be where we are, but we also know we worked hard for it and never gave up.

6. Is there anything else you'd like to add based on your experience?

Just be sure to go into your location independent career for the right reasons. Don't use travel as a way to run away from problems. Having a career, a circle of friends and a life at home is a wonderful thing. You need to go into a life of travel because you love constant change. We don't mind not knowing where the future takes us, in fact, we thrive on that. But it's not for everyone. And it doesn't magically make things better. Problems and insecurities follow you around no matter where you are. So if you do decide to become location independent, make sure it is because you love seeing the world and are comfortable not seeing your friends and family a lot. We love every minute of it, but we know and understand that it's not for most people.

CHAPTER 9

TRAVEL HACKING

Travel hacking was one of the reasons I was able to do the first three years of my trip with just over $60,000 total. That total amount is really small compared to all the places I visited (over 76 countries) and experiences I had. If I were to divide that amount per year, which is $20,000 on average, it is way less than what I used to spend *just* to live in New York and even Puerto Rico.

So, in case you don't know what travel hacking is, I'm going to show you some basic terms and tricks that will help you get started on this "art" of travel and get you on the way to becoming a travel hacking ninja.

WHAT IS TRAVEL HACKING?

Travel Hacking is the "art" of traveling for free or with a small budget by accruing rewards, chasing miles and discounted fares, and looking for every possible way to "game" the system. The goal is to spend as little as possible to have travel experiences that would normally cost much more.

In the last few years, I've earned over 1,000,000 miles and points without flying, in addition to the thousands of miles earned flying around the world.

BASIC TRAVEL HACKING TIPS

Travel hacking takes time to master and a lot of patience, but with these 30 tips you can begin to understand what travel hacking is and how you could save money on your upcoming trips.

1. Sign-up to your favorite airline and hotel's rewards program

One of the most important elements of travel hacking is accumulating points or miles to redeem them for free travel or upgrades. Think of miles and points as a currency, and just like any currency, they do have a specific value. Some miles are worth pursuing while others are not.

If you don't know which programs would be best for you, start by creating a frequent flyer account with American Airlines (One World), United Airlines (Star Alliance), and Delta Airlines (SkyTeam). These three airlines are the best ones to cover all three major airline alliances, giving you greater chances of earning and redeeming miles. While these airlines are US based, signing up with them still works well for travelers from all around the world.

For hotels, sign-up for the Starwood Preferred Guest program. This is a hotel program that gives you points for hotel stays, and it also lets you redeem some airline miles for such stays.

2. When looking for airfares, don't just stop at the first site you visit and buy the airfare there

Usually, I start with Kayak.com since it is a pretty good aggregator, and it includes most airlines. But, after reviewing the prices there, I like to compare them with the Google-ITA Matrix to see the "actual" fare published by the different airlines. You can't buy the tickets at the ITA Matrix site, but it helps to know how much it should cost.

Then I head to skyscanner.com, which for some reason, more often than not it seems to show the cheapest flights with the best routes. (This is currently my favorite site) After that, I like to keep digging deeper on the Internet by searching on sites like momondo.com, travelocity.com, expedia.com, smartfares.com, and orbitz.com, among others. Sometimes they offer exclusive discounts that can make the airfare even cheaper than on the actual airline's site.

3. Start searching for flights leaving on Tuesdays, Wednesdays, and Saturdays

In general, search for flights departing on Tuesday or Wednesday as these are generally the cheapest days to fly. Saturday is often cheap too since most people don't want to break their weekend to fly.

4. Be very flexible with your travel plans

Flexibility will help you get the cheapest airfare possible. Look for flights at "inconvenient" times like early in the morning, late at night, and red eyes (overnight flights). Also, use the search tool in Kayak.com and other sites that show airfares three days before and after your desired date to see if there are cheaper days to fly near your preferred dates.

5. Is your destination flexible too? Play and choose your destination based on the airfare your find

Sites like Kayak and Skyscanner make it easy for you to explore the world and decide on your next destination based on the cheapest airfare they find from your city of origin. If using Kayak, visit kayak.com/explore and put your departure city, desired month or season in which you want to travel, and any other specifications you'd like to add. Kayak will show you a map of prices spread all over the world indicating how much it would cost to go from your city to that place.

Skyscanner, on the other hand, allows you to do this from their search page, where instead of putting a specific destination, you can write "everywhere" and select any given month or the whole year. Then, you'll see a list of countries, going from cheapest to the most expensive, along with their estimated airfare.

6. International airfares are often the cheapest when booked 54 to 66 days in advanced

Some studies show that this timeframe is a good rule of thumb to buy your international flights, but exceptions always happen. Domestic flights are usually at their lowest about a month before the trip.

7. Still, booking things last minute can save even more money

If you're really flexible and don't mind planning your trip within the last couple of weeks or days, you could save a lot of money by purchasing highly discounted rooms, tours, and trips that have not sold at their regular price. Many companies prefer to make a lower profit over none by selling them last minute at a lower rate.

For last minute cruises you can check CruiseSheet.com, for hotels there's the HotelsTonight.com app (iPhone, Android, Windows), and for tours, GAdventures.com and IntrepidTravel.com both have highly discounted last minute tours all around the world.

8. Be open to a stopover

Tickets that include them are often cheaper. When you fly direct, you are probably flying to or from the airline's hub, which makes it a bit more expensive. When you have a stopover, prices tend to be lower because you usually pass through the airline's hub, but don't stay there.

9. Don't rule out budget airlines

These airlines can be huge money savers! Thankfully, a bunch of budget airlines like Air Asia, Norwegian Air, WOW, and EasyJet, among others, fly cheaply from the US to Europe, Asia, and even Africa. They do the same thing as other carriers –getting you from point A to point B– but at lower costs and sometimes with fewer amenities than regular airlines. From my experience, I happened to save over $300 by flying from Bangkok to New York with Norwegian Air instead of any other major carrier. And in Asia, I've flown with AirAsia for as low as $35 one way. Seriously! In Wikipedia you'll find a page with a list of all budget airlines categorized by base country. (Search for "list of low cost carriers.")

10. Fly to Alternate and Secondary Airports

Many cities have secondary airports, and more often than not, these serve low-cost carriers. Low-cost carriers, or budget airlines, are cheaper since they pay lower landing fees and offer fewer perks than the bigger airlines. But generally, these airlines are a good deal.

Usually, these secondary airports are far from the city center, so be sure to check how easy it is to get from the airport to the city center, and how much it would cost you. In some cases, this local transportation cost can make a cheap budget airline fare more expensive and less time effective than a major airline.

In addition, you can combine major airlines with Low-cost carriers to reduce your airfare total price (for example: Flying from New York to London on a major airline and from London to Frankfurt on a budget airline). You can check low-cost-airline-guide.com to see all the budget airline flight options in Europe. Or, you can check the Wikipedia page mentioned before with the list of all budget airlines in the world. Simply look for your destination on the list and see which airlines fly there.

11. Be open to including some overland travel on your trip

You might want to visit Bratislava but find that it is too expensive to fly there. Luckily, Vienna is just an hour away by train, so why not fly to Vienna (which will probably be cheaper) and take the train to Bratislava? Overall, even with the train, your trip could be cheaper than if you flew to Bratislava directly.

You get the concept, right? If your destination is expensive, search for other major cities close to it and search for flights to those places. Then, search for overland travel options (bus, train, car) to your final destination.

12. Don't forget to visit the airline's site directly

Sometimes, the prices shown in the aggregator sites don't necessarily match what the airline show's directly on their site, and in some cases, visiting the airline's site might save you some money.

13. Visit the Airline's International Site (of a different country from your own). In other words, "fake" your location.

Depending on exchange rates, a flight may be cheaper in the airline's local site and own currency. (i.e. Asiana Airline's (a Korean airline) Korean site instead of their US site)

It is also possible to book a flight on a website located in another country that is neither your base country nor the airline's base country (for example, the Canadian website for a US airline).

International Airlines can offer different prices on their international websites based on the current exchange rate. In this case, the exchange rate can either help you a lot or hurt you; so make sure to calculate it properly.

Even search engines like Skyscanner allow you to visit any of their international sites, and each of them shows a different price since each site has different airfare providers. For some reason, in many cases I found the Italian version of Skyscanner to be cheaper than their US version; but, there were a few cases in which the US site was cheaper. Just, play and have fun searching on several international sites. How to do this? When you visit Skyscanner, or other search engines that have international sites, you'll often see a little flag on the top right corner of the page (or bottom, in some sites). Click on it, and select the country, currency, and language of your choice. Then, search for your airfare!

14. Are you a student? Get your discount!

If you're a student, or if you have 26 years or less, you could benefit from some discounts exclusive to students. The best sites to check for these discounts are STATravel.co.uk, StudentUniverse.com, or other student-oriented travel agencies for more information. Just be sure to have a current student ID since it will be required.

15. Even if flying round trip, consider searching your flights as two one way tickets

Sometimes, searching for the same route as two one-ways instead of a round-trip can cost less. While search engines tend to mix airlines to give you the lowest price, this not always the case, especially when budget airlines are an option (yet are not shown in many search engines).

16. Even if only flying one way, consider looking for your flight as a round trip

It might sound contradicting to what I just said above, but quite honestly, the airline industry makes no sense when it comes to pricing. So, even if all you want is to fly one way from one city to another, also check for the airfare as a round trip since sometimes it could be cheaper as a round trip. You simply don't have to take the flight back.

You wouldn't feel bad about ditching your return flight since it cost you less than buying a one way, and in some cases, you could call the airline and they could either give you the credit for the flight or change it to a different date in the future (should you think you might want to use it). This, of course, depends heavily on the terms and conditions of your airfare. This technique might not work as well in the US, but the airline industry in Europe is completely different, and in certain occasions this works well there.

17. Consider splitting your bookings between domestic and international flights

Let's say that you're flying from Tennessee to Paris, with a layover in New York City. After you know the price of the trip, search it again by searching the domestic leg (Tennessee to NYC) and the international leg (NYC to Paris) separately. In many cases, this technique proves to be a huge money saver. While domestic fares don't tend to vary that much, especially if it is a popular route, international fares do vary drastically, and often when they are paired with a domestic flight they tend to become much more expensive.

One example is when I bought a multi-city flight from Milan to New York, to Puerto Rico, to New York, to Brazil, and finally to London. When I searched the entire trip, the total cost was over $3200. But, when I split the domestic leg, which is the New York to Puerto Rico round-trip, the total cost came at about $1,500 ($1,250 for the international flights and $250 for the NYC to Puerto Rico round-trip). It's not even half the original price!

18. When possible, avoid airline hubs as your destination by purchasing a "disposable" onward flight

Every airline has a hub airport (or a few). When you fly with an airline to its hub airport, chances are your airfare will not be the cheapest since airlines charge more when your final destination is their hub. Let's say, for example, I want to fly from New York City to Charlotte, North Carolina. Probably, the first choice I'll see on the search engine will be US Airways (since Charlotte is their base). But, what if I searched for a flight on US Airways from New York City to New Orleans? Since Charlotte is their base, most probably they will make a stop in Charlotte and make me chance flights to go from Charlotte to New Orleans. In many cases, this flight combination will be cheaper since you're bypassing the hub, not staying there. But here's the fun part. Who says you have to get on the Charlotte to New Orleans flight? You can just get off in Charlotte and ditch the second leg.

There are four conditions for doing this, though:

- Only do this if your final destination comes out cheaper as a "layover" to any other city en route.

- You can only do this if you *don't* check bags (only carry-on bags). Should you check in your bags, they will go to the final destination.

- Should you decide to do this internationally (i.e., Buy a flight from Bangkok with layover in Kuala Lumpur and final destination in Sri Lanka... but get off in Kuala Lumpur), make sure you have all the required visas and documents to be able to stay in such country.

- Do not mention your plans to stay in your "layover" city to the airline's staff, as they will consider this practice as "fraud." This is not illegal, but airlines don't like it because technically you're gaming the system (which is the whole idea behind travel hacking)

Skiplagged.com is a site specifically dedicated to finding these "layover" fares for you. Have fun with it! From my experience, this site will work best for US domestic fares and some European ones.

19. Wikipedia can help!

Not satisfied with the airfare prices you've found on search engines? Head to Wikipedia! Not all search engines show budget airlines (which we know by now are usually the cheapest ones). So, if you know your destination's airport name or code (i.e., LAX), go to Wikipedia.org and search for the airport there. Wikipedia usually shows all the airlines that fly to the airport, including the obscure/unknown ones, and the destinations covered by those airlines. Once you see an airline on the list that didn't appear on a search engine, go straight to their website and check the prices there.

20. Use the "incognito" or "private browsing" mode found on Firefox and Chrome browsers

When you're checking airfares one the Internet, websites keep track of your visits through cookies, and often, they raise the prices (or keep them at the same price if it recently went down) simply because they know you've already visited the site and saw a given price. Incognito mode hides your browsing history and cookies so that sites don't know it is you again.

21. Sign up for credit cards when they offer a substantial sign-up bonus - like 30,000 to 50,000+ miles or points

While travel loyalty programs have gotten more restrictive in the last few years, it's still pretty easy to get a big miles bump through the use of credit cards. Many travel-branded credit cards offer sign-up bonuses as high as 50,000 points, which can equal a round trip to Europe or even up to two domestic round trips in the US. Usually, to earn the sign-up bonus you need to spend a minimum amount of money in a certain amount of time. To achieve this, you can use your credit card to pay all your daily spending like gas, groceries, rent, online shopping, etc. But, make sure you pay your balance every month to avoid paying interest rates on your purchases.

22. Cash in your miles and points for flights and hotel nights

Even if you don't apply for new cards like the one's mentioned above, it's possible you have a few miles and points here and there with your current credit cards. As I mentioned before, miles and points are a form of currency, and like any currency, their value changes with time (in this case, it tends to devaluate). For that reason, you should have an ideal target of amount of miles you need for flights or X amount of nights in any given hotel, and once you reach that target, use your miles to save some good money. Sites like FlyerTalk.com and Reddit.com/r/churning can guide you through the best ways to use your miles.

23. Buy gift cards and pay with them

Often credit cards offer 2X – 5X points per dollars spent on specific stores (i.e. office supply stores, drug stores, etc.). These stores often sell gift cards for restaurants, gas stations, online shopping, and more. Buy these gift cards (only for stores or services you already use) with your credit card so you can rack up multiple points per dollar. Then use the gift card to pay for dinner, gas, or whatever necessary purchase in the applicable store.

24. Do a Mileage Run to gain Airline status and add miles to your account at a low cost

Mileage Runs are when people take flights simply to earn miles and elite status. They look for last-minute deals or fare specials and hop on the next flight. The truth is that with all the latest changes in the airline industry, Mileage Runs are becoming harder and harder to do, but still, now and then you find a good one. To learn more about how to do mileage runs and find out when these deals happen, check the FlyerTalk forum. (Note: Their jargon can be a bit advanced)

25. Stay in more than one hotel in a city

Several hotel chains offer promotional rewards for a certain number of "stays". This means that if you're in a city for four nights, you could stay at four different hotels to accumulate four "stays". Sure, moving every day is not ideal, but this is a fast way to accumulate free nights very fast!

26. Multiply your miles by shopping online

When shopping online, search for the products you are interested in buying through your airline of choice mileage mall portal (for example, If you're accumulating United Airline miles, then you go to their MileagePlus Shopping). Most major airlines have an "online mall" and they link to it on their website or frequent flyer page. These "online malls" often offer multiple points per dollar or specific bonus miles (i.e. 5,000 extra miles) for certain purchases.

You might not always find the products you're looking for in these shopping portals, but it never hurts to search for them to see if there's any option to earn multiple miles! A good site to check for current rewards is evreward.com.

27. If the first person can't help, try someone else

Sometimes asking nicely by phone or at the hotel or airline's front desk or check-in clerk for an upgrade, freebie, or discount is a good way to travel hack your vacation. Often you will get a "no" for an answer, but the best thing to do is hang up or wander around the hotel/place and come back again when the staff has changed (or call back). More often than not, the answer is highly dependent on who you talk to and often staff are more than happy to give you that bigger room, business seat, or other perks if they will go to "waste" otherwise.

28. Understand and use the sharing economy

This might not apply to flights, but travel hacking extends beyond flying cheaply. And these days, sharing is a big part of saving money on the road.

For accommodation, you have the option of "crashing" on someone's couch through Couchsurfing.com for free or renting a room or apartment with AirBnB.com at a fraction of what a hotel would cost. Or, you can even camp at someone's backyard with

CampInMyGarden.com.

If you want to share a car ride from one city to another, there's BlaBlaCar.com (mostly UK), Carpooling.co.uk (in Europe), and Kangaride.com (in the US and Canada).

Or, if you want to have experiences delivered by locals, and not necessarily by tour companies, you can book experiences through Vayable.com, WithLocals.com (only in Asia), or homemade dinners through EatWith.com.

29. Take advantage of repositioning

If transatlantic or transpacific airfares are pricey, look for a repositioning cruise. These cruises take place twice a year as cruise lines move their ships from the Mediterranean to the United States, or from the Caribbean to Western Europe, or from Alaska to East Asia, and so on. These cruises are sold at dirt-cheap prices since the cruise company prefers to gain a profit from that trip rather than to travel with an empty ship.

30. Finally, stay on top of any travel hacking news and low fares by following the best in the industry

Currently, ThePointsGuy.com is one of the best sites, if not the best, when it comes to learning about travel hacking, finding deals, and earning more miles through tricks and current offers. Also, ChrisGuillebeau.com shows a few travel hacking tips and deals on his site too.

Lastly, I want you to understand that miles and points are a currency, and just like any other currency, they can devaluate. So, always have an amount goal of miles in mind to be able to get any given flight for free, but once your reach that goal, use the miles. Don't accumulate your miles just for the sake of accumulating, because in the future they will probably devaluate and give you a lower return for your efforts.

Also, be aware that miles in certain frequent flyer programs expire after a year or a year and half of inactivity. So, if you flew using your frequent flyer program, then your miles will be good for another year (or so, depending on the program) after your last activity. But, if you're using a credit card linked to your frequent flyer program, any purchase made with your credit card that gives you points or miles, is also considered as an activity. So, if you feel like you won't fly for a long time, then just head to any coffee shop and buy a drink with your credit card to extend the expiration date of your miles.

I recommend keeping track of all your miles using AwardWallet.com. It is free, and it allows you to add all your frequent flyer and credit card accounts (with miles/points) to know your total miles and the miles' expiration date on each account.

Of course, this is just the beginning of your travel hacking "career", but by applying these tips and more for 30 minutes every couple days or so, soon you could earn over 100,000 miles/points without actually flying that much or spending high amounts of money.

HOW TO FIT EXPENSIVE DESTIONATIONS INTO A BACKPACKER'S BUDGET

While travel hacking concentrates mostly on flights and hotels, it can also be used on your every day spending and experiences on the road. It's all about carrying on the same "travel hacking mentality" into every single spending.

I'm a strong believer that backpackers should not limit themselves to destinations that are easily traveled with small budgets. As a backpacker, I've traveled to expensive destinations like Maldives, Japan, Australia, and Hong Kong, among others; and still managed to do them with a reasonable backpacker budget.

I'm going to show you several tactics I use on a daily basis to keep my travel costs down to a minimum.

Travel Hack Your Trip With Hotel And Flight Points/Miles

This is basically what I already explained in detail at the beginning of this section. Accumulate miles and points in your favorite airline and hotel loyalty program to use them to your advantage. Redeeming points/miles for free flights and stays will help substantially to lower your average daily spend.

Look For Accommodation Alternatives Beyond Hotels

Also mentioned briefly before, consider renting a room or apartment through Airbnb or similar site. If you're staying in the same city for a long period, some accommodations give a lower weekly or monthly rate. Hostels are also a great and popular alternative to paying less for accommodation.

Lastly, if you'd like to go the free way, check for Couchsurfing hosts at your destination. Couchsurfing is a travel social network where people from around the world open their home to offer a place to stay to a fellow traveler, for free.

Scout For Small Cafes And Street Food Stalls

Often, when I go out to eat, I walk around for a few minutes looking for restaurants. If I'm not satisfied with restaurant prices, I start looking for small cafes and then for street food stalls. Street food will more often than not be the cheapest option (and in many occasions the most delicious).

Think Of "The Spillover Theory"

Guidebook recommendations are often nice, but sometimes establishments deteriorate their service or raise their prices after they gain "guidebook fame." Should the recommended hotel or restaurant not fulfill your expectations, think of spilling over to an adjacent hotel/restaurant. Usually, these adjacent locales absorb the extra clientele (the spillover) of the popular place and often provide the same service for a lower price.

Buy Groceries At Supermarkets And Local Morning Markets

If you want to eat cheap, you have to buy food like a local. Go to the local supermarket and buy produce and food you can cook at your place. Morning markets are excellent for buying fresh produce and other locally produced foods at cheaper rates. You just have to be a morning person!

Have Your Best Meal At Lunchtime

Many restaurants in major cities offer a lunch menu at a fraction of the normal price. These lower prices are often reserved to a time block (i.e., 11 am to 2 pm) and sometimes apply to carry-out/pick-up food only – it varies per restaurant. When I find these cheaper lunch menus, I try to have a generous lunch so I can have a smaller dinner, which would hopefully cost less than a full I'm-very-hungry dinner.

Be A "Late Customer"

Many convenience stores, supermarkets, bakeries, and coffee shops offer some of their remaining perishable merchandise at a percentage of the price when it is near closing time. Businesses want to still make a profit out of the unsold donut, cupcake, cooked pasta, etc.; instead of throwing it away as a loss. To find out of these sale prices/times, ask the cashier if they have any sales at some point of the day.

On the other hand, certain businesses offer an "early bird" discount to boost business activity early in the morning.

Be Aware Of Local Attractions Schedules (When Is It Free?)

Many museums, bars, and attractions are free one day of the week or month. Some attractions don't charge to enter their facilities for a certain period of the day while they might charge later in the day when it is busier or when the main event happens. Ask around in tourist information booths and request specifically for the *free schedules* of local attractions. Otherwise, search online for "free things to do in _____" to see all your options.

Use Apps To Guide Yourself

I use apps like TripAdvisor, Tripomatic, and Trover to know which sites are around me and get a brief description of what it is about. With these apps, I've guided myself through the city, hopping between sights, without the need of a guide or tour.

Take Free Walking Tours

Many major cities offer free walking tours around the city center. Take advantage of these since they are often very insightful and sometimes even better than paid tours. These tours are often run by people who love their city and enjoy showing it to visitors.

Ride Local Transportation

This is a must. You must ride like a local to save like a local. If people take buses to go around the city, you should do it too. If they take trains or trams, do take trains and trams too. Think like if you were living here, how would you go from A to B on a recurring basis without spending much?

Buy Attraction Passes

Several major cities that have expensive attractions offer bundle passes or a "city card" that allows you entry to several attractions at a fraction of the price. Buy this only if you know you'll visit enough attractions to make it worth your money and the savings.

Lastly, I want to conclude by emphasizing that to travel cheap; you have to think like a local. Think like this is the city you live in, so how would you explore it routinely without spending much?

No matter where you go, there you are.
– BUCKAROO BANZI

ESSENTIAL TRAVEL APPS, CHEAP AIRFARE AND ACCOMMODATION RESOURCES

EXCELLENT SITES TO FIND CHEAP AIRFARES

The following are all sites I use.

Kayak.com: Great starting point for searching cheap airfares, especially if you are based in or departing from the US.

Skyscanner.com: More often than not one of the cheapest sites, especially if your flight involves budget airlines that Kayak might miss.

Momondo.com: This one is great for international flights. Like Skyscanner, it is also often the cheapest sites since it crawls directly through airline (as well as hotel, car rental, and vacation package) sites rather than utilizing a third-party aggregator.

Vayama.com: Great for international flights outside the US. Sometimes it is way cheaper than other sites, but sometimes it is also more expensive.

AirfareWatchdog.com: The site has several ways of searching for flights, from search and compare of different sites, search from your departure point or search to an arrival city. They also have a page that shows you the top 50 fares from around the world at that moment (though it mostly focuses in US departures or domestic flights). I highly recommend signing up for fare alerts for your desired location/dates, or if you're simply browsing, follow them on Twitter to get fare tweets.

Hipmunk.com: When searching for flights, Hipmunk shows you a timetable with colored bars ranked in descending order of "agony," a factor devised to incorporate price, flight duration, number of stops and departure/arrival times.

Matrix.ITASoftware.com: I love this site since it is the backbone of many online travel agencies and airline websites. While you can't book your flights here, you can check the real price of flights according to what is presented by the airline, not the search engine (like Expedia and others). This is my measuring tool to know if I'm getting a good deal somewhere else or if prices are just ok. Or sometimes, I use the Matrix first and then try to replicate my findings in another flight search engine to purchase it.

Google.com/flights: Google purchased the licensing rights to ITA Matrix back in 2011, and now uses the technology to power its own flight search site. Best suited to searches for domestic U.S. flights since it doesn't search as wide an array of airlines for international flights. Google Flights' map view allows you to drag and drop your chosen route to another destination to see how the fare changes, while a bar graph view lets you see how fares rise or drop over a set time.

Adioso.com: Designed for budget-conscious travelers with flexible itineraries, Adioso allows you to conduct flexible itineraries —like "New York City to Asia in late April for

15 days"—and get a good idea of where you can go and for how much. You can also sign up for email alerts and see if the price drops.

OTHER AIRFARE RELATED SITES YOU SHOULD KNOW OF

@TheFlightDeal on Twitter: The website for The Flight Deal serves up fare deals with some wanderlust-stoking visuals, but to maximize your time, a quick scan of their Twitter feed (and the common hashtag #Airfare) will tell you everything you need to know about the best up-to-the-minute, round-trip and tax-inclusive fares to/from just about everywhere in the world.

Mileage Run Deals forum on FlyerTalk.com: This site is for serious travel hackers! Devoted frequent flyers share their best fare-finds here, using a shorthand of airport codes (e.g., MIA, LAX, JFK, SJU, etc.) and airlines (DL for Delta, UA for US Airways, AA for American) and abbreviations like rt (round-trip), ow (one-way), and ai (all-inclusive of taxes and fees). You'll often find suggestions about the best and worst days to book, as well as good rates of return on award bookings and fast-track tips to elite status. Learn the lingo of this insider forum to get the most out of it.

Yapta.com: A partial cure for travel buyer's remorse, Yapta lets you know when your already-booked fare gets offered for less elsewhere, and when (per each airline's individual policy) you're eligible for a refund equal to the discount. When a fare drops within 24 hours of your purchase or dips low enough to offset the airline's change fee, Yapta sends you an alert that you should rebook at the lower price, pay the change fee, and pocket the difference.

Flightfox.com: This site is like a 21st-century version of a travel agency. Here, instead of you searching for your flights, you pay a fee that starts at $49 (rising with the complexity of the challenge) to have an expert search for a highly discounted flight by searching all the loopholes possible to get the absolute cheapest airfare possible.

EXCELLENT ACCOMMODATION SITES I USE

Agoda.com: It has a good inventory and often with lower rates than other sites.

Airbnb.com: Great to rent apartments/homes or rooms from short and long term. They have a large inventory and is often the cheapest compared to similar sites.

Booking.com: In my opinion they have a better inventory than Agoda and sometimes they are even cheaper.

Hotwire.com: They have their "secret hot rate hotels" list, which gives you hotels for a much lower rate without telling you specifically which hotel is until you get it. It's not scary since hotels tend to be good. They also have regular hotel rates.

Priceline.com: Different from Hotwire, Priceline allows you to bid the price for a hotel stay, allowing you to save money.

Hostelworld.com: This hostel site has the largest inventory and availability. I use it quite often.

HostelBookers.com: Quite similar to Hostelworld, but sometimes you find cheaper hostels here.

Couchsurfing.org: Couchsurfing helps you connect with people abroad to sleep on their couch or extra bed for free. But the site is not just for that, it's also to meet people and explore with a local.

Expedia.com: I don't think it is the best search engine these days, but now and then they can surprise you with a really good hotel or airfare deal, so worth checking.

ESSENTIAL TRAVEL APPS

Beyond the apps directly related to the sites mentioned above, I also use some essential apps that help me stay on top of my "travel game".

AwardWallet – Excellent to keep track of all your frequent flier and credit card miles and points.

TripIt – I use it to keep track of all my travel plans. I just email my flight or accommodation confirmation to the app, and it organized it beautifully on the app, adding reminders on my calendar to not miss anything!

Google Maps – Essential to move around anywhere.

Trail Wallet – For me, this is the best app to keep track of my spending on the road. It keeps me on budget by being a conscious spender.

Word Lens – This app translates anything from one of its supported languages (Italian, Portuguese, Russian, Spanish, French, German) into English (or vice versa). But, the cool thing is that you just need to point your camera to the word or phrase to translate, and it does it live on the screen!

Trover – This app is pretty cool to see pictures people have posted of things that are around you. Sometimes I get to discover pretty cool sights, restaurants, and other stuff I wouldn't have found out otherwise.

TurboScan – I use this app to scan any important document and turn it into a .pdf by just taking a picture of it.

SpeedTest – A good Wi-Fi connection is essential for my work, so before committing to pay for any hotel or stay at a coffee shop, I test the Wi-Fi speed with this app. This app saved me from renting an apartment with awful Wi-Fi!

Xe.com – Keeps me up to date with the current currency exchange and helps me convert any currency pair.

Tripomatic – Pretty cool app to use in any major destination. It shows all the attractions around you on a list or map, with a brief description and photos. Helps me organize my trips according to the sights I see around. It's kind of like being my own travel guide.

Around Me – Looking for the nearest pharmacy, supermarket, gas station, or other locale? Around me will show that to you.

TripAdvisor – Similar to Around Me in terms of how I use it, but Trip Advisor has reviews that help me know if the restaurant, hotel, etc., is good or not.

Snapseed – Excellent free app to quickly edit and enhance some of my iPhone shots.

Mint.com – This app helps me stay on top of my finances by having an overall picture off all my accounts in one place.

Skype – This is essential to stay in touch with friends and family, plus to make important calls too.

Whatsapp – Free text messages to anyone in the world using Whatsapp!

TPG to go – The Points Guy app is pretty cool to know which is the best credit card to use in the stores around your location to see which one will give you the most points per dollar spent. Also, it shows you current travel deals and more.

Do something wonderful, people may imitate it.
– ALBERT SCHWEITZER

CHAPTER 10

PACKING

Depending on the type of traveler you are and the kind of business you might be running on the road, you might need to select a specific kind of luggage to carry all your belonging and equipment properly.

Options range from hard case luggage, duffle bags, backpacks, daypacks, wheeled backpacks, camera bags, and so on.

I admit that I am biased to recommend a combination of a backpack and a daypack. They offer versatility and comfort when moving around. Backpacks are flexible, light, and resistant to long-term travel; and a daypack is great to keep your equipment to keep your business running. These days, backpacks and daypacks come customized to carry safely equipment like laptops, cameras, lenses, and so on.

Most location independent entrepreneurs I know use backpacks and daypacks, so it is possible you might fall into that category too. (I do!)

This is just a recommendation; in the end it is up to you to choose what you feel it is best for you.

CHOOSING THE RIGHT BACKPACK

Since I travel with backpacks, specifically a Gregory Imlay 22 as a daypack and a Gregory Z40 as a backpack, I'm going to tell you all you need to know to select the best backpack for you. I recommend both of my backpacks. They are light, sturdy yet flexible, and comfortable to fit on any body size.

So, if you'd like to be as happy with your backpacks as I'm with mines, here's what you should consider:

Size

Your backpack should be comfortable enough to allow you to carry at least 20 to 30 pounds (9 to 14 Kg). It should be proportional to your body; the shorter you are, the smaller your backpack fitting should be. Why is size really important? Not only because it will dictate how much you can carry with you, but also because a correct sizing proportion between body and backpack helps balance the weight properly. This reduces back pain or topping over due to weight.

When trying out different backpack sizes, you should ask a sales representative to put some weights inside the pack, so you know how 20 to 30 pounds (9 to 14 Kg) feels like on your back.

Also, size dictates if you can take your backpack as a carry-on on your flight or not.

Material

You should try to get a backpack that is waterproof or at least come with a water resistant cover (that you can put over the bag in case of a downpour). One of the worst things that can happen is getting all your things wet while running under the rain. Also, the material should dry quick enough to prevent creating a bad "environment" inside your bag.

Structure

Backpacks come with internal and external frames. External frame backpacks tend to be bulky, ugly, and have rods sticking out that can get caught on anything along your way. And who would want that? These days, you should buy an internal frame backpack. Internal frames tend to look better, be lighter, and more comfortable.

Loading Method

Many backpacks are top loading (you get everything from the top) but these are not the most efficient in terms of searching for stuff. If you need to get something that is packed at the bottom, you have to take everything out first. A good option is to have a front panel loading backpack. These have a zipper along the length of the backpack that allows you to get into any part of your backpack without much difficulty. My Gregory Z40 is top, bottom, and frontal loading, making it very convenient.

Lockable Zipper

Make sure each compartment of your backpack has two zippers that can be locked together.

Multiple Compartments

This helps organize and separate your things better.

Padded Hip Belt

Since most of your pack's weight is going to be carried on your hips, make sure that the hip belt is padded to make the weight support more comfortable.

Padded Shoulder Strap

This makes carrying the load much more comfortable as your pack will be pushing downward on your shoulders too.

Sternum Strap

This strap helps bring the weight forward by connecting the two shoulder straps over your chest. It also helps to distribute the weight and relieves your shoulders from some of the weight, saving you from some excessive shoulder pain.

Contoured/Padded Back

Lumbar shaped packs make carrying the load much easier as they help distribute the weight more evenly. Some even provide some space between your back and the back of the pack to provide for some "breathing space" along your back. This reduces your sweating on your back.

Style

While style is the least important factor when selecting a backpack, let's face it; style plays a big part in your decision-making. Just keep in mind that while you choose something you like in terms of design, it should also be efficient and comfortable. If not, your "fashion statement" will cost you some headaches and back pains along your trip.

Price

Of course, the price will play a huge part in your decision-making. Just have in mind that backpacks range from $50 to $300+ and that not necessarily the most expensive pack will be the best pack. You will see that a $100-$200 pack can do better than an expensive pack if it fits all your needs.

Daypack

Probably, you will travel with a backpack and a daypack. Daypacks are much smaller and are used to keep all the things you need accessible during the day (and even things you rather not leave alone in your backpack – like your passport). When carrying both packs at the same time, the backpack is carried on your back, and the daypack is often carried in front. Carrying both packs this way might look weird, but it helps balance the weight on your body. You'll see it is a common practice among backpacker to do this.

TIPS ON PACKING

As a general rule, you should not carry more than 30% of your weight, or at least that's what the Boy Scouts told me when we went camping. I'll stick to that for now. But, I'll be honest by saying that I'm breaking that rule at the moment. My backpack weights around 24 pounds (11kg) when full and, funny enough, the smaller daypack weights around 29 pounds (13kg) (that's because of the electronics). I weigh around 130 pounds (60kg), so if you've made the math, you'll see I'm a few pounds over. Ooops!

Some additional tips to consider when you're packing:

- If you're traveling in cold weather, try packing clothes that can be used in layers. Layering is more effective that carrying that bulky sweater and coat. And layers can be mixed and matched, so you look as if you have many styles throughout your trip using only a few clothing elements.

- Choose dark or neutral colored clothing. This helps "hide" the dirt and stains.

- Roll you clothes into tight tubes. This saves space and reduces wrinkling.

- Put an odor absorber or dryer sheet inside your pack, it will keep your clothes smelling fresh.

- Carry a laundry bag in your pack. It will help separate your dirty clothes and keep your clean clothes fresh. If traveling long term, you'll do laundry on the road, so with the laundry bag it's easier to do this task.

- If you have travel guides, photocopy only the pages you will need. Don't carry the whole book as they take so much needed space and add unnecessary weight to your back. Plus, these days you can carry these guides in digital form instead of paperback.

- When writing your packing list, try to reduce things to the minimum. Don't add things just because you think they can come in handy. From experience, most of the time those "handy" things are almost never used; and you ended carrying them all the way. No matter where in the world you are, chances are you'll be able to buy whatever you need at any given moment.

- Use airtight bags for your clothes and important stuff. They help to reduce the amount of space clothes take and also help to protect everything from getting wet.

- If possible, try to leave at least 25% of your pack free. You will see that as you spend your time traveling, it will fill up with souvenirs and extra stuff.

- Use a waterproof cover to protect your backpack from the rain.

- Last but not least... Pack everything you think you will need and then get rid of half of it. This is just a rule of thumbs to help you pack only the essentials. In fact, the saying goes, "pack half of what you think you need and take twice the money you think you'll spend."

WHAT I CARRY IN MY BACKPACKS

Whatever you carry for your trip is highly dependent on your travel style, where you go, and what your business is. But, here I want to show you what I've been carrying for the past three years. Every product listed below is essential to my travels in one way or another, and I recommend every one of them since I use them pretty much to live on the road.

My Daypack: a.k.a. "The Office"

Gregory Imlay 22: This daypack is big enough to use on long hikes, like Kilimanjaro and the Inca Trail, but small enough to use on a daily basis while in the city. In it, I carry my computer and electronics.

What I carry in it:

Macbook Pro 13" Retina: I just love Mac. The power and performance it has is way better than what any small netbook might have. It's great for heavy editing of videos and images without losing processing performance.

iPhone 5: I use it to stay on top of my social media, emails, blog, google maps directions, and what not. This is honestly one of my most essential tools since these days I do pretty much everything with my phone.

Nikon D5200 with an 18-105mm Lens: One of my goals is to produce good quality pictures that record and tell the story of my travel experiences. With the Nikon D5200, combined with the 18-105mm lens, I've been able to improve my picture's quality significantly. This DSLR combination is a good start for any traveler that wants to take great photos without having to carry too many lenses or equipment.

Sigma 10-20mm f/4-5.6 Lens: This lens is great for wide angle photos and landscapes.

Nikkor 50mm f/1.8D Lens: Part of improving my photography is being able to play more with depth of field as well as being more creative with composition and how I shoot things.

Sony Cyber-shot DSC-TX10: When doing adventurous activities where the DSLR is not ideal to take, I choose to carry the Cyber-shot since it's easy to handle, small, takes really good shots, and it is waterproof!

Western Digital My Passport 2TB Portable External Hard Drive: I use it as a backup and as extra memory. One thing you learn while on the road is the ridiculous amount of Gigabytes pictures can consume. Plus, if anything happens to my computer, I have a backup of everything in here.

LaCie 1TB External Hard Drive: Yup, apparently 2TB are not enough for me. I chose LaCie because just like Western Digital, these hard drives are compact, light, resistant, and reliable.

Kindle E-reader: This has saved me from countless hours of unproductive boredom on trains, planes, and buses... or simply anytime I feel like reading. It's light and slim, so it's easy to carry.

Dark Energy Portable Backup Battery: These days the battery life in most devices is pretty slim, or am I just using them too much? Anyway, this small battery, about the size of an iPhone 5, can charge your iPhone up to 5 times with one full charge, and charge up to two devices at once.

GoPro Camera: I might not use it as much as I would love to, but I find it useful to create time-lapse and get some cool wide angle or action shots.

Ikea Egg Timer: As dumb as it sounds, I do carry an egg timer with me all the time. No, I don't cook eggs, but this timer is perfect to create rotating time-lapse shots with the GoPro since you can place the camera on its flat top and let it rotate freely.

Petzl Headlamp: I use it for extreme things like caving and for mundane things like having a spotlight when camping or walking at night on an unlit street. (yes, that happens now and then)

Moo Business Cards: Hey, I have to promote my blog! These cards are of great quality and cheap. I love them, so I recommend them.

x-mini Speaker: I love to amaze people with the sound quality of this mini speaker. Any time I'm traveling with friends or in a group, there's always the chance to play music out loud. This speaker always delivers...

Dynex Travel Adapter Plug: This all-in-one converter has worked perfectly for me, and it is not too big, so it's easy to carry.

Charmin Travel Toilet Tissue: I always carry these! Small packs, so they fit anywhere, and they have saved me a few times I've had nature's call in the most undesirable places (just think, Africa!).

My Main Backpack: a.k.a. "The Closet"

Gregory Z40: This backpack is super streamlined, so it is light and resistant. I've found that 40L is big enough to carry everything I need for long-term travel while still keeping my load on the lighter side. It has well-padded straps, a sternum strap, and hip straps, as well as a comfortable and ventilated back padding. Seriously, this backpack is really good.

I used to travel with an Osprey eXos 58, which is really good too, but I prefer to force myself to travel light than to have more space, thus, weight.

What I carry in it:

Icebreaker T-shirts: Icebreaker t-shirts are designed with the active traveler in mind, so they are light and "smell resistant". Sometimes it's hard to do laundry on the road, either because of lack of time or facilities, so it's good to have a few of these.

Ex-officio underwear: This underwear is really good for travelers and active hikers since they are light, comfortable, quick dry, and are made with "smell resistant" fabric.

Sea to Summit Tek Towel: This camping towel is small enough to carry but good enough to dry me properly. Plus, it dries itself pretty quick.

Eastern Mountain Sports Rain Jacket: This is ideal to have if you're into hiking or if you're visiting a destination in its rainy season.

Craghoppers hoodie jacket: I carry one Craghoppers jacket that comes with mosquito repellent integrated into the fabric (safe on the skin), protects against UV rays, and is quick dry.

Travel-Size Toiletries: I have a small bag where I carry enough toiletries to last a couple weeks. These include everything from personal hygiene and styling to vitamins and meds. I simply buy them as I need them wherever I am.

Smartbag: I learned from experience that it's good to have all your clothes and electronics safely stored in airtight travel bags (at least while in transit). While any bag can do, I've found Smartbag to be very good, resistant, and durable. They've helped keep everything dry when I get caught in the rain or when my backpack gets thrown out of a boat into the sea (yes, that did happen once).

First Aid Kit: Again, another thing I never fail to carry and this one I also learned from experience after I had an accident at an archeological site in Honduras where no immediate medical assistance was available. My first aid kit is small enough to fit anywhere in my backpack, but it has all the essentials to treat any common injury.

12 t-shirts: In addition to the Icebreaker t-shirts, I have regular t-shirts for everyday life. Including the Icebreakers, I have a total of 12 t-shirts. And, if they have cartoons on them, I'm in!

10 underwear and socks: In addition to the exOfficio underwear, I have regular underwear, mostly Calvin Klein underwear and Puma socks.

5 short pants: These shorts I've bought along the road, wherever I find a good pair that I like. These include swimwear.

1 pair of jeans: Yes, I do carry jeans. A regular pair of jeans from American Eagle.

1 pair of Havaiana flip-flops: These, by far, are the most comfortable pair of flip-flops I've ever owned.

1 pair of Puma sneaker: I've always liked Puma. They are light, comfortable, and look good with most type of clothes.

If you wonder where to buy backpacks and travel gear, you can find them at your local adventure shop, Amazon.com, and in the US I also recommend REI.com (one of the biggest outdoor sports stores nationwide).

The tragedy of life is not so much what we suffer, but rather what we miss.
– THOMAS CARLYLE

IN THEIR OWN WORDS

MARCELLO ARRAMBIDE

Originally from: United States

Website: WanderingTrader.com and
TheDayTradingAcademy.com

1. What did you do before traveling (particularly to make a living) and what made you decide to become location independent?

I was day trading in the mornings and also working for a bank. I started to take a few trips and eventually ended up spending about 3 weeks in Argentina. Since that was much longer than my normal trips I knew that I could actually start traveling around the world so I decided to come back quit my job and then day trade full time.

2. How did you deal with different aspects of becoming location independent? (emotionally, socially, and financially)

It just takes a little effort. Once you decide to go there is no coming back. Once I decided that I was going to live this new lifestyle I decided that I wouldn't give it up. To make friends I would make sure to be more social and attend meetups to be able to meet people. I was already day trading so I didn't need to worry so much about money. The real deal came when I had the pressure of making money in the market. It just took some adjustment but eventually I got used to it.

3. What prompted you to choose this specific path of income and how did your previous job help you get there?

I have been day trading for about 12 years and had my job just as a security blanket. My previous job allowed me to have the security to know that I was able to do this long term.

4. How do you evaluate your current situation (financially and emotionally) compared to your "past life"?

I would say that I live a much better quality of life than I did before. I can make my own rules, travel anywhere around the world, and have and make enough money where I don't have to worry about money. I don't have to sit in rush hour traffic two times a day. It is a much higher quality of life which is what I always wanted.

5. If you had to do it all over again, what would you change?

I would have quit my job earlier and started this life much earlier.

6. Is there anything else you'd like to add based on your experience?

Most people think they want this life. They think they want to have their freedom. Most people however, don't think about the work that goes into having this quality of life. It is definitely worth the risk because not everyone can live this kind of life.

Anyone can choose to live this life and take that risk and it would be 100% worth it.

SECTION 4

LIVING THE DREAM

*Your time is limited, so don't waste it living someone else's life.
Don't be trapped by dogma – which is living with the results of
other people's thinking. Don't let the noise of other's opinions
drown out your own inner voice. And most important, have the
courage to follow your heart and intuition. They somehow already
know what you truly want to become. Everything else is
secondary.*
– STEVE JOBS

CHAPTER 11

PUTTING EVERYTHING IN ACTION

Before I jump and start talking about life on the road, I want to make sure you know all the steps and have a clear path to achieve that lifestyle by giving you a macro outlook of the whole process. So, here's sort of a quick start guide laying out the steps that will allow you to become location independent and be able to spend much less on long-term travel.

Step 1 - Ask yourself a series of personal questions.

This is the most important thing you must do before deciding on anything. Ask yourself *why* do you want to become location independent and *how* would you like to achieve it. Do you have a specific purpose? Ask yourself all the questions I presented in Chapter 1 to see where you stand and if location independence is for you.

Step 2 - Define your location independence by defining you own micro-business

If you feel confident you want to do this, define your path to location independence by choosing the best way to finance your lifestyle, as described in Chapter 2 and Chapter 3. Make sure you choose to base your micro-business into something you're passionate. Also, do your best to make it online too, since that's part of the key to this whole lifestyle.

Can you translate your current job or profession to a location independent lifestyle? How can you accomplish this in your given situation?

Take a look at the micro-business ideas in Chapter 4 and see if any of them suit you, or if you should modify any of them to fit you best. Or who knows, you can come up with something completely different!

Step 3 - Become a travel hacking ninja

Rack up frequent flier miles (without necessarily flying) to pay for your initial travel expenses. The time it takes to build up enough miles for a one-way ticket to anywhere in the world is usually a couple of months (especially if you take advantage of the huge credit card sign up bonuses). Use AwardWallet.com to track your miles.

In addition to racking up miles, follow the travel hacking tip mentioned in Chapter 9 to find flight deals and get dirt-cheap hacker fares for flights and hotels.

Step 4 - Save, save, save money

Focus on saving money to cover enough time to live location independent, or at least to cover your first 6 to 12 months of business and personal expenses. I give some effective tips on

Chapter 6 to save money like crazy!

Step 5 - Choose a "Location Independence Day"

Establish a point of no return by buying that first airfare to anywhere in the world. Use your frequent flyer miles if you have enough. Buy the flight at least a few months in advance to give you time to organize everything, travel-wise and business-wise. That Location Independence Day will become an exciting milestone in your life, and a source of encouragement to work hard and make everything work once you have it set on your calendar.

Step 6 - Plan your time abroad

Where will you go, what will you do, how will you get there, how will you move around... Do your best to understand each destination you're planning on visiting to know exactly how you could live, travel, and work there – as explained in Chapter 3 and Chapter 8. And even more important, how much would it cost you. Is it sustainable for you?

Step 7 - Tie up loose ends

Get rid of everything you don't need for your new lifestyle. Sell it, donate it, toss it. Establish some technical services to help you stay on top of your travel and business game and to have everything organized back home. See the end of Chapter 8 for more on this.

Step 8 - Live it!

Don't rush out and try to see all the sites once you arrive at your destination. Remember, you're not on vacation, you're now location independent! You have Freedom. You have time.

Welcome! Relax, and enjoy this new chapter in your life!

_____

It's a dangerous business, Frodo, going out your door. You step onto the road, and if you don't keep your feet, there's no knowing where you might be swept off to.
– J.R.R. TOLKIEN

_____

CHAPTER 12
LIFE ON THE ROAD

This section is dedicated to teach you more about certain logistics to make the best out of your life (and money) while being location independent, plus how to deal with certain situations that are simply part of the "travel package."

It doesn't matter how much you've read of any given destination and how much you've prepared yourself to be there, there's always an element of surprise that might come through culture shock or simply an "ah, I didn't expect this to be this way." That's part of the beauty of travel!

SETTLING SOMEWHERE NEW

No matter how much or how little you prepare yourself to go to a new destination, these are a few things you should always do once you arrive in a new place:

- Find the nearest local supermarket and buy enough food to last a few days. Usually, you can find them easily as you roam around town, but in any case, you can ask any of the locals in the area or use Google Maps to search for it. You should also familiarize yourself with the locations of ATMs, banks, restaurants, and pharmacies.

- Find the nearest hospital, medical center, or doctor's office just to be familiarized with its location in case of an emergency.

- Purchase a local SIM card to be used in your unlocked phone. Most countries offer affordable pre-paid plans with 3G internet.

- Learn a few basic words in their language to ease your communication, or if you want to learn their language properly, book some language lessons during your spare time.

- Write down your address and emergency phone numbers on your phone.

UPS AND DOWNS ON THE ROAD

People might think that the life on the road is all peaches and cream, puppies, and piña coladas. Well, it can sometimes be, but in addition to those beautiful moments, you need to be aware that life on the road can be as tough as life back home. And in some cases, you will need to know how to deal with it.

And with that, I'll start with loneliness...

How to Deal with Loneliness on the Road

More often than not I travel by myself, so people tend to ask me out of curiosity, "Don't you get lonely?"

The truth is, when I venture the world by myself, there are times when I do feel lonely. No matter how well I prepare myself to be alone while on the road, that lonely feeling has its way of sneaking through the crack. I guess this is normal.

There are times when I also travel with other people, and guess what, loneliness also makes its way through every now and then. Loneliness is not about the amount of people you are with; it is an attitude.

But, I don't see my lonely feelings as a bad thing. They are part of the independent travel experience, and I have learned to deal with them and still feel comfortable, even when that sad feeling sinks in.

Embracing Loneliness

First and foremost, I embrace the feeling. Throughout life, I've learned that the things you fight against the most are the ones that keep coming back. So, why not embrace it and produce something positive out of it?

Sometimes being lonely makes me reflect on things in life. It helps me to learn about myself, what I like, don't like, and so on. Often, marinating in the feelings for a while allows me to see things I wouldn't otherwise pay attention to. It's like I'm looking at things at a slower pace.

Sometimes this sparks my curiosity, making me question things to try to understand them from this different perspective. Why not? This can be an opportunity to absorb new things and experiences openly and almost vulnerable.

Being Creative

This lonely feeling can also serve as a source of inspiration to create something meaningful – something of value. In many cases, I channel those feeling into being productive; whether it's writing a post, drawing something, or just brain-vomiting any idea that gets sparked by the moment. I love moments like these because creativity flows naturally.

After a while, not only the sad feeling fades into the background by itself, but a sense of accomplishment steps in after seeing the creative product of this feeling. In the end, I feel so empowered that nothing seems to be impossible.

Being Proactive

Sometimes being proactive in other ways helps dwindle the lonely feelings. For example, at the beginning of every trip I do my best to prevent the jet-lag effects by being active. Jet lag can bring down even the seasoned traveler, and the sad and lonely feeling sinks in.

Getting busy enough and challenging myself –tasks, sightseeing, events– often keeps me motivated, ergo the blues (almost) don't sink in.

Traveling solo doesn't mean I'm alone, just like traveling with friends doesn't necessarily make me feel part of the crowd. Even when I'm not a social butterfly, making friends on the road has been pretty easy for me, enough to give me some company now and then, resulting in great friendships in many cases. Hostels are great examples of friendship breeders, and even long bus rides like the ones I took in Guatemala. Sitting 10 hours in a bus from Antigua to Semuc Champey, and a quick hi, was all it took to get to know other travelers that eventually became my companions for the rest of my trip. It never hurts to say hi!

Do Some Outreach

Search online for local groups of people with similar interests and see when and where they meet. Searching for local Facebook groups is an excellent option, or you can also participate in a Couchsurfing meetup if there's one in your current city.

Should you feel you're an expat in the city you're in at the moment, focus on meeting other expats through the same options I mentioned before. They will share their views and experiences of the city, and possibly help you ease your transition and develop your life there more comfortably.

Not always a physical companionship is needed for company

Sometimes, just a simple Skype call can be an instant boost to your morale. Thanks to technology, online friends have become ever more present in this society that now they have as much influence as "real/in the flesh" friends. We are so connected through the internet that these virtual friendships don't feel as shallow as they once used to feel. At least I feel that way... And there's no better place to reinforce this idea than in the worldwide travel blogging community.

Sometimes loneliness comes, and I can't do anything about it or with it, but that's ok still. Usually, the benefits of being out there in the world outweigh any lonely feelings that might come. In those cases, I just let the feeling be. It won't last forever, right?

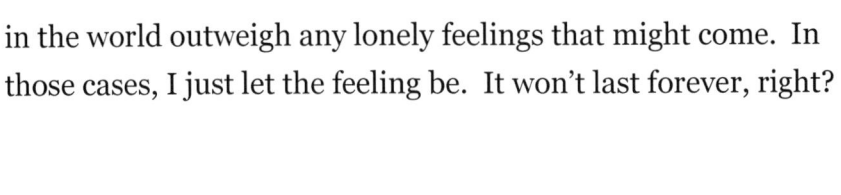

Do. Or do not. There is no try.
— YODA

STAYING HEALTHY

You should always look after your health, especially after flying across several time zones, which alters your usual biological routine. This change can cause physical stress and make you feel under the weather.

Make sure you catch up on missed sleep and give your body some time to adjust to all kinds of new foods you're subjecting it to (unless you used to eat the same back home) in order to have a healthy start in each destination we go. As one of my dear readers said to me through Facebook; "health is really wealth." (Thanks, Lisa!)

I completely agree with Lisa, since without our health we wouldn't be able to do anything to the fullest expression.

Eating Habits

Regarding food, you know your habits, allergies, diets, and restrictions. Take those into consideration and see how they affect you at every destination you visit. For example, I am allergic to soy (it's not chronic, but it can get bad enough to make me commune with the toilet for a few hours). So, whenever I visit a country where soy is a major ingredient in their cuisine (Japan, China, and several other Asian countries) I either try to eat dishes with the least amount of soy. Or if I have no choice, I will eat any soy containing option and plan for the possible need of going back to my hotel after dinner. It doesn't always happen, but I keep that option open in case my body decides to react to it.

Jodi, of LegalNomads.com, is quite open about her Celiac Disease and how she copes with it on the road. The most interesting thing to me is that even though she has this condition that doesn't allow her to eat gluten, she's one of the most popular and respected foodie travel bloggers out there. A disease or a physical limitation doesn't mean you need to limit yourself in what you really want to do. On the other hand, you should think that your limitations have no power over your goals, or use them as an advantage to focus your intentions or to stand out from the crowd (if you are doing something public, like a blog).

Medications

Should you have a chronic or non-chronic disease that requires you to take medication on a recurrent basis, you should prepare yourself to be able to keep your health on top while traveling.

Depending on the length of your trip, before departing, you should ask a doctor for a prescription for X amount of pills/medicine to last for the entire trip. Not all doctors are willing to give larger than normal prescriptions, so there's a chance you might need to explain your situation to the doctor. Should the doctor give you the entire prescription, you should also ask him for a letter that proves you are carrying all that medication legally. This is in case you get stopped at immigration and get questioned for the meds.

Should the doctor not give you the entire prescription for the trip, ask him for the name of generic alternatives you could get in another country, or the active ingredients of your medication so you can go to a proper pharmacy or hospital and ask for medication made for your illness and with those ingredients.

I, for example, was diagnosed with Crohn's Disease over 13 years ago. During those years, I had several ups and downs health wise, with some of the downs sending me to the hospital for surgery. A year before I left New York City to do my trip, I had a big concern about my health, especially since during that year I underwent a medication process similar to chemotherapy that required me to visit the hospital every two months for IV therapy.

Luckily, my health improved dramatically after a year in treatment, though I still had to take some prescribed pills when needed (when I felt my digestive system was reacting wrongfully to something I ate). For my trip, I packed enough of those pills to last for at least a year, and funny enough; I think I can count on one hand the times in which I actually took the pills in the last three years! Thankfully I haven't had the need to use them much, but I feel "safe" knowing that I have my medication with me in case I need it.

Foreign Pharmacies And Doctors

If you're in a country in which you don't speak the language (especially if in a developing country), try to restrict your medicinal purchases to well known or franchised pharmacies/drugstores or to only visit travel doctors (doctors who specialize in treating foreigners). While they might be more expensive than the mom-n-pops stores, you will have a better chance of actually getting what you need and not worry that the medicine you get is something that got lost in translation and could probably hurt you instead of helping you.

As an example, a close friend of mine had a spider bite on his foot on the way to Cambodia. After his foot had got swollen enough that prevented him from walking, he went to a random pharmacy where people didn't speak any English. He did his best to explain the situation with body language and eventually got his medicine. He applied it as indicated and hoped for the best. The next day his foot was even worse! Not being able to contain the pain, he decided to go to a travel doctor, which officially indicated him that the medicine he got at the local pharmacy was the wrong one and caused the infection to get worse. He got better in the end after the doctor prescribed the proper medicine, but he (and I) learned from that experience to always check the active ingredients and see how they treat the symptoms.

Physical Limitations

You know your body and what it is capable of doing. So, why not plan a trip that gives you the best of what you want without pushing your physical limits? My entire family once planned a ski trip to Vermont (which I missed, unfortunately). The ages in the group ranged from 60s to early teens. My mom, being the oldest in the group knew very well she would not ski. Not only was she not physically able to do it, but also it was not in her interest. Still, this didn't stop her from going on a ski vacation! What did she do? She did some light hikes around the ski lodge, she visited the city and enjoyed the history and culture, and she relaxed on her own while the other rolled down the slopes. She still enjoyed the trip since she did what she knew she would love doing.

A dear reader of my blog, Lisa (who I quoted before), is currently planning a trip around the world but is highly concerned about her health since she is hypertensive and very sensitive to heat and freezing water. My recommendation to her was not to see this as a limitation, but as a way to plan her trip accordingly.

My recommendation to her is to avoid high altitude places, at least for longer periods, and to plan her trip according to the seasons. Should she not want to be under extreme heat, why not spend the months of March to September on the southern hemisphere while the rest of the year on the northern hemisphere? This will help her avoid the highest temperatures since in theory she'll be in "fall and winter" the entire year, which doesn't necessarily mean cold weather because she could travel to places that are closer to the tropics.

Mental Health

Traveling long term, especially if you're constantly moving and doing everything on a budget, can become frustrating at some point. You will get tired, you will feel like you don't want to see anything else, and you will get psychologically unstable. It happens. The way I treat this is by either changing the scenery or changing the pace.

I'm a budget traveler at heart, but sometimes I need to splurge a bit to keep my sanity. I will spend a few nights in a nice hotel, go out for a few nice meals, or pamper myself with a spa or whatever I crave for. This helps me keep mi sanity.

Or, I simply slow down my pace and stay in one city for a long period (a couple months or more). Having a base helps you develop certain social relationships with locals you might crave, establish a routine, and give you free time to do things outside travel. Also, during this time my craving to travel reemerges, which prompts me to plan the next leg of my trip. But now, I'm always conscious that I travel best when I spend a few months traveling and a few months based somewhere.

Keep Doing What You Love Outside Travel

Love to read? Keep reading as much as you can. Love to photograph or film videos? Do that too! The point is to take time for yourself to have some moments of peace in which you concentrate on doing the things you love.

Stay In Touch

Hearing your mom or that special someone's voice is priceless, and these days it is extremely easy to do no matter where in the world you are. Skype is the most common tool these days, but even Google Voice and Facebook allow you to call people for a small fee or even for free!

Keep Some Form Of Exercise

You don't need to pay for a gym membership to exercise. You can walk or jog around the park, visit a free open-air exercise park, or simply do a quick exercise routine in your room. I recommend reading NerdFitness.com since it focuses on the best ways you can stay fit and has an excellent post on staying fit on the road.

Don't Forget Your Vitamins

While I'm not the most responsible person vitamin wise, I still have to recommend you to take your vitamins to supplement any minerals and nutrients you might be missing on the road due to a change in diet, or simply to keep a healthy balance of vitamins in your body.

SOCIAL LIFE

One of the things I love about traveling is the ease of making new friends on the road. Sometimes you meet that new person on a train, an airplane, a hostel, a street, or anywhere. As travelers, we tend to be very open-minded and welcoming with almost anyone friendly enough to interact with us. We love to create that sense of community with fellow travelers and that sense of connection with non-travelers.

One of the things that help us make that connection with other travelers is our shared passion for traveling, our ability to exchange our stories, and the possibility to share our current and future journeys with them.

I admit that for me it's easier to make friends when I'm traveling solo than when I'm traveling with close friends or a partner. When traveling with a group of friends it's easy to ignore other travelers because you are focused on spending time with your friends. In many cases, groups tend to portray a sense of exclusivity, keeping other travelers from interacting with you. But when traveling solo, you normally express a certain openness that tends to charm people, making it easier to establish a conversation, a travel partner, a friendship.

Traveling has given me the chance to make friends in many ways, from the most common to the most unusual. Some of these have become good, long friendships, while others have been ephemeral. With some of them, I have been able to create a bonding in a way I have never done with some of my life long friends. But I think I get where that bond comes from... We share a passion, a desire, a goal, an ambition. We love to share the past while looking at our future journey. We want to see the world and get the best of it.

So that you know... I'm not a social butterfly; in fact, I'm a very shy person. But, traveling has pushed me forward and helped me overcome that "social obstacle". One of the most memorable road friendships I made was with my good friend Milena when we met at a hostel in Warsaw. It was a straightforward hello that took us on a long walk through the Old Town and gave us many hours of great conversation. We clicked in seconds, like if we knew each other from before. Today we still keep in touch and exchange messages about future travels.

I think my craziest friendship was forged while I got lost in South Korea's subway system. I was completely lost in translation and had no idea how to buy the ticket. It was Saturday at 5 am and no one was around. Then suddenly I met these three Americans –Christopher, Alyssa, and Julieth– who were as lost as I was, so our obvious reaction was... "Let's get lost together." We ended up spending our time together in South Korea and after that we skipped to Thailand. We had an amazing time in Bangkok before continuing on our separate paths. Up to this day, we still get together from time to time in New York and Berlin.

I have learned that the opportunity to make new friends while on the road can come at any moment. You just have to be open enough to accept it and willing enough to develop it. Some friendships will work out while others will just be a short companionship. But no matter how long or short you keep that friendship on the road; one thing is for sure, they form a valuable part of your trip, of your destination, and of your travel experience.

Traveling Solo, with a Partner, or as a Family

I've mostly traveled solo and love it due to the freedom I feel when deciding on what to do next. I only need to think about what I want, so as long as I do what I really want, I'll be a happy person. Sure, I have moments of loneliness, as I wrote before, but those fade away as soon as I get proactive and meet other travelers or focus my attention on something else.

Having said that, I've also traveled extensively with a partner or friends, and this is a completely different travel experience. Here, things are no longer "about what I want," it is more about "what we want" or "what can we do together." There are moments in which you might need to sacrifice some of your time to do something not necessarily on top of your list. There are other moments in which you will want to do something, yet realize that you'll not be able because it conflicts with your partners plans or not work at all in the overall plans you have together as a couple or family (and vice versa with your partner or family).

Still, the fact that you are traveling with a partner or family doesn't mean you have to do everything together. After all, you're all different people with different interests.

Yes, you might do something you're not necessarily interested in doing for the sake of spending time with your partner during your trip (and he/she might do the same), but this is only healthy if there's a balance and a limit. Should this happen too often, this could bring some tension into the relationship and possibly ruin part of the trip. Instead, it is good to sometimes give yourself some "me" time and do what you really want without "forcing" your partner to do it too (if he/she doesn't have that interest).

Also, when you're on the road with your partner, you spend 24/7 together, so having some solo moments are necessary to keep your sanity and respect. So, don't be afraid to do things on your own now and then.

To this day I haven't traveled with kids, since I don't have any, but I know of several location independent families that don't use their kids as an excuse not to travel or do what they really want to do while on the road. For example, Caz and Craig of yTravelBlog.com have been traveling the world together for over 15 years now. They now have two kids, but they didn't let parenthood stop them from traveling the world. In fact, they are now more inspired to travel than they had ever been before. Currently, they've been traveling all Australia as a family, driving a campervan from point to point, experiencing the best things the country has to offer. What about their kids' education? Simple, homeschooling.

A New City, a New Life?

When you start living in a new city, chances are things will be completely different than back at home. Depending on how different, it could either bring some cultural shock or just a mild adjustment.

Just because the place you're based now is different, doesn't necessarily mean your lifestyle will be completely different too. I've found that my life is quite similar in various places I've lived in as a digital nomad. It is still me –the same person– in essence, so I will still desire to have similar routines or to do similar things I like as long as they are available where I am.

I've found that keeping some habits also helps make a new place feel more like home. For example, if you used to go to the gym, why not look for a gym in your new city too? I've found that keeping some consistency in the things you used to do back home helps with the adjustment process of the new place since you feel more at peace with the things and routines you're familiar with.

SAFETY

Traveling, as anything in life, can have some risks involved. We always question ourselves, What if "blank" happens? Well, there's always a "what if..." on our mind but if we are cautious, we can prevent those "what if's" from happening and have an amazing time on the road.

It doesn't matter if you're traveling alone, with friends, or with fellow travelers you met on your way; there are basic precautions and approaches you should try to keep your trip as safe as possible while still having a good time:

- First and foremost, be cautious. We all want to explore everything, but use your common sense. If you see a desolate area that doesn't seem too safe, stay away from it, or at least don't go by yourself. If you have a local host at your destination, have them go with you; they might know how safe or not the area is. Also, try not walking by yourself on dangerous-looking alleys or late at night.

- Be as friendly as you can, but don't be a simple open book. If hanging with fellow travelers you met on the way, no matter how friendly they are, keep in mind that they are virtually strangers. So, be careful what you share with them and how you share it. For example, don't just share with random people the exact location of where you're staying. (This could potentially be a mistake if an undesirable person hears it and decides to "pay a visit" to steal your things when you're not there. I've seen this happen before.)

- You should be alert and pay attention to your surroundings. That includes people too. Always keep an eye on your stuff, so you don't become an easy target for pick-pockets and thieves.

- When in Rome, do as the Romans do... I know you've heard that one before. Right? Well, the phrase says it all. By doing this, you will not attract too much attention to yourself by unknowingly insulting a different culture. For example, when in Middle Eastern countries, women should probably cover their hair in public places (and definitely in religious grounds) as a form of respect to their culture and religion, and as a way to not attract too much undesired attention.

- Try being inconspicuous. Of course that big backpack on your back doesn't help achieve this, right? But, when not carrying your backpack try looking as less touristy as you can. It's kind of cliché to have that tourist look by wearing the "I love NY" (or whatever destination) t-shirt and by wearing that big flag patch from your country on your bag. You know... dress as you would normally dress back at home and dress appropriately for the place you're visiting. (i.e. sacred places, museums, etc.).

- Females... while there are certain countries people might recommend you to avoid as a solo female traveler due to their cultural and religious view towards "single western females," truth is that if you are a respectful traveler, chances are nothing will happen to you. In many cases, the "dangers" you might face there are the same or less than the dangers you faced back home. Check the current situation at your destination, especially towards females, and decide whether it is smart for you to go solo or if it's better to have company. Since I'm not female, I highly recommend following and reading these superb female travel bloggers who have traveled the world extensively and can speak about the subject much better than I can. These are AdventurousKate.com, LegalNomads.com,

RunawayJuno.com, and NomadicChick.com.

- There's nothing better than being confident while traveling. This is key to any traveler. Be confident or at least fake it. Act like you know where you are even if you don't. Even though there's nothing wrong with getting lost, flapping your map in the middle of a crowded street will attract some attention, especially the scammers' attention. Doing that just makes you an easy target. So, if you need some directions, ask someone (still with confidence) or go inside a store or café and peek at your map.

- Always be polite. Not only it's good manners but also a way to have a good standing among other people. Don't offend the locals with rude and crass behavior. You don't have to "a saint," but at least have a common sense of behavior.

So, these are just some "safety and approach" tips that will help you have a fun and amazing trip while being safe and cautious. Being cautious is not about restricting yourself; it is about having common sense. *Exercise it!*

IN THEIR OWN WORDS

JODI ETTENBERG

Originally from: Canada

Website: LegalNomads.com

1. What did you do before traveling (particularly to make a living) and what made you decide to become location independent?

I was a corporate lawyer in NYC.

I didn't decide to become Location Independent. I quit my job to travel for a year, starting a blog. When the blog became popular, I started to receive paid offers for freelance writing, and I figured "hey, let's see where this goes!" Seven years later, it's still going :)

2. How did you deal with different aspects of becoming location independent? (emotionally, socially, and financially)

I was lucky to have met many people who were doing the same around the world. They've been constant sources of support and advice, as well as great hugs.

Financially, if I wasn't saving money I wouldn't be doing what I do. I'd have gone back to being a lawyer. For now it works! You can see the details of my income streams on my about page.

3. What prompted you to choose this specific path of income and how did your previous job help you get there?

I did not choose it. I started my site for my mother to see what I was up to when travelling. It chose me.

My previous job as a lawyer is useful insofar as I do not need to hire a lawyer for basic things like contracts or registering trademarks. And of course thinking of things as a lawyer would (mitigating against potential problems) does coming in handy! It also means you worry a bit too much ;)

4. How do you evaluate your current situation (financially and emotionally) compared to your "past life"?

I like myself a lot more as a person now. That might just be a factor of getting older, not just because I'm no longer a lawyer. I love that I learn new things every day, that so much of what I do involves connecting through food, and reading about history of food.

Financially I make a lot less. I also spend a lot less.

5. If you had to do it all over again, what would you change?

I would have gotten onto Wordpress earlier, instead of blogger. And I would have learned how to code.

6. Is there anything else you'd like to add based on your experience?

I think many people assume you are running from life by doing this kind of thing. There are definitely people who are. But ultimately, by building a business in a flexible environment, I have continuously pushed the boundaries of who I am, learned new things, and met great friends in the process.

SECTION 5

SETTLING BACK

To travel is to take a journey into yourself.
— DANNY KAYE

CHAPTER 13

POST TRIP

PLANNING FOR CONTINGENCIES

While the intention behind this guide is to help you create a location independent life, I'm aware that not everyone is looking to do this for the rest of their life and will probably want to reintroduce themselves "back into society." There's also the reality that some people, as hard as they might want this and work for it, might not be able to reach the point of being fully sustainable on the road. Or simply, they realize that a location independent lifestyle is not for them.

So, if you're ready to go back home or if it didn't work for you, what now?

First and foremost, be proud of yourself for taking the leap of faith, trusting in yourself that you could do this, and for enjoying your time on the road.

Here are a few things you should consider beforehand to create your "return home plan:"

- Keep enough money in a separate savings account to cover your airfare back home and about a month of accommodation. (You can keep this money in any account, as long as you're conscious of not using it)

- Stay in touch with a close friend or family with whom you can stay for a couple weeks right after you return to your home country.

- Have a credit card with enough available balance should you need to use it in an emergency.

- Look for medical insurance that will cover you back home.

- Find a lawyer, accountant, or any professional advisor that will help you manage your personal business and other affairs now that you're operating back in your home country.

- Have your resume ready before heading back if you're planning on looking for a job.

THE BENEFITS OF YOUR TRIP

Now, how can we turn your experience on the road into something that can help you reintegrate into the career and life you used to have back then?

Use your travel as a learning experience. It is possible that on the road you obtained new knowledge and skills that could make you a more valuable asset; whether you're looking to create or continue your business, or looking for a high paying job. Life on the road can teach you so many things like problem-solving, adaptability, people skills, open-mindedness, confidence, networking, decision-making, and more.

Even if you didn't learn all these skills at school and don't have a diploma stating how you got them, you can still show you got these skills by presenting yourself professionally during your interview and if possible, show how these skills helped you on the road and life in general. Inspire your prospective boss with your experiences and all those empowering benefits of travel. Or, why not inspire yourself to continue to be your own boss to have the time and financial freedom to travel whenever and wherever you want?

Use Your Travel As Your Internship

Whether you have your micro-business or are simply traveling for the experience and the freedom, you should use this time of your life to improve on yourself too. How can you improve your career prospects with your travel experiences?

This will take a bit of research on your part. If you've made up your mind you want to settle back and reenter your career, give yourself a few months before your time on the road ends to prepare yourself. Investigate about other people on the career ladder who are right where you'd like to be, and see what they did to get there? Do they have skills you still need to gain? Why not use your time and experiences on the road to improve on these?

I recommended this resource at the beginning of the guide, but these days you can learn so much through free online college courses like the ones presented in Coursera.org. Take your time, study, do the tests, and gain knowledge.

What are your weaknesses? Can travel help you strengthen these? Yes? Then plan your experiences on the road to do this.

Before your time on the road ends, why not try a working holiday where you can gain even more skills? I talked about working holidays before, so you can check Chapter 5 to understand better this option.

Start Networking Yesterday

When it comes to work, any work, networking is key to getting a better position or having more options. MeetPlanGo.com is an excellent site for people looking to do a career break and looking to re-enter their career after their break. I like how they say that "a break is career defining, not career defeating." I also believe this to be true.

Even when I've been out of the traditional architectural office for over three years now, I've still gotten job offers should I wish to return to New York in the near future. As nice and comfy as that feels, I'm still not ready to go back to that.

Your Trip and Your Resume

Can you "pimp" your resume with your travel experiences? Sure you can, but wait, think professionally. Don't add that you bungee jumped in New Zealand or surfed in Bali (unless you're applying for a job directly related to extreme sports). But, if you volunteered, taught English abroad, or did a working holiday, why not add these experiences, the skills learned, and the deliverables you achieved during your time there?

As much as you might like to add everything you learned, still keep your resume focused and on point to the kind of job you're applying for. If you think what you learned in your working holiday has nothing to do with this new prospective job, keep it out of this particular resume, or simply add the experience as a blurb at the end of the resume as "extra skills and experiences."

Meet, Plan, Go has an interesting article about "Getting Back to Reality and Resumes" that you might enjoy reading.

Finally, I recommend to be proactive a few months before coming home by sending your updated resume to companies of your interest, that way, you might have the chance to make a quick and smooth re-entry.

EASING YOUR RE-ENTRY

Re-entering doesn't have to feel as depressing or stressful as many people think it should be. Here are a few tips that might help you with it.

- Should you get sad about being back home, it's ok, let it out as it will pass.

- Look back at your trip through your collection of memories: pictures, souvenirs, memorabilia, etc. Relive those moments and think of how you felt back then.

- Share your experience with your friends and family. Also, share your newly acquired knowledge of the world and more to inspire others to get out there and see the world.

- Stay in touch with new friends from your travels through email, Facebook, and even in person if they live nearby.

- Don't stop learning. If you learned a new skill on the road, like making spring rolls in Vietnam or tango dancing in Argentina, why not continue using those skills back home by practicing them or keep improving them by taking more courses? Or, find groups with these similar interests and socialize with them. If you live in a big city, it is possible that there will be a group for that, and you'll probably find them on Facebook if you search for them.

- Keep meeting new people back home. Find the expat group in your city and hang out with them. Or, mingle with travel groups from meetup.com or couchsurfing.org during their social gatherings. It is always good to hang around with like-minded people who have gone or are going through similar experiences as you did while on the road.

- Become a Couchsurfing host to still keep in touch with your traveler side by showing people around your city. Plus, if you couchsurfed during your trip, it is always nice to return the favor.

- Volunteer your time with something travel related like the free walking tours in your city or something along that line. You can also volunteer your time at a local Youth Hostel.

- Finally, don't let your adventurous spirit die and plan your next trip!

Perhaps travel cannot prevent bigotry, but by demonstrating that all peoples cry, laugh, eat, worry, and die, it can introduce the idea that if we try and understand each other, we may even become friends.
– MAYA ANGELOU

CLOSING THOUGHTS

Deciding to become location independent is a big life changing decision that shouldn't be taken without proper thought and preparation. But, now that you've read this guide you have greater knowledge on how to achieve it.

Having said that, as much as I could have written here and told you everything step by step, this guide is worth nothing if you don't act on it. There's not just one way of becoming location independent, as you saw already, so it is possible you might choose a path not covered here. Still, you can pick and follow the concepts and aspect you feel apply to you. But, no matter which path you choose to take, make sure it is something you're passionate about. I'd like to quote Deb of ThePlanetD.com by saying:

> ...if you follow what you love, you have a better chance of financial freedom.

I hope this guide helps you reduce the learning curve to enter this lifestyle of travel or to live life on your own terms. You'll see that once you start exploring the world, you'll meet like-minded people who will serve as support, inspiration, and even as friends. And not only that, but you'll realize that there was nothing to fear about this, except your own fears.

But in the end, the most important thing is to take that first step towards the life you want. I'm sure you won't regret it in the end.

Ohh, and hey... the world awaits!

Sincerely,

Norbert Figueroa

P.S. If you have any questions or concerns, feel free to email me at norbert@globotreks.com with the subject "Location Independent Questions." I'll be more than happy to help answer them or to give you tips about your journey.

Also, why not share your story? I would love to feature it in any future edition of this guide.

If you have any comments about this book or feel like it is missing something you'd like to have covered or needs to be improved, shoot me an email! I'm all ears!

Finally, word-of-mouth is crucial for any author to succeed. If you enjoyed the book, please leave a review on Amazon. Even if it's just a sentence or two. It would make all the difference and would be very much appreciated.

P.P.S. Don't forget to download your free worksheets: http://www.globotreks.com/worksheets/

ABOUT ME & STAY IN TOUCH

A quick blurb about me

Norbert Figueroa is an Architect from Puerto Rico who hit the pause button on his career in 2011 to travel the world for one year. That year-long trip is still going on these days, with no set end date. His goal is to visit all 195 U.N. recognized countries by 2020.

Get in Touch and Follow the Journey

- http://www.globotreks.com
- https://www.facebook.com/globotreks
- https://twitter.com/globotreks
- http://instagram.com/globotreks
- http://www.pinterest.com/globotreks
- http://youtube.com/user/globotreks

Printed in Great Britain
by Amazon.co.uk, Ltd.,
Marston Gate.